REFLECTIONS

'Batts from Barming'

The life and times of George Batts, MBE, Ld'H.

Notes on the cover -

Front cover – George in Jerusalem Cemetery; a Cemetery he invariably visits when in Normandy whether on an 'official' tour or on a private visit.

Back cover – Gold Beach; George looking at where he landed on D-Day.

Batts from Barming –

The subtitle of the book derives from George's working life and the play on words of where he has lived since moving to Barming.

Barming is a civil parish in the Maidstone District of Kent. It lies to the west of Maidstone, the county town, and had a population of 2,234 persons. The eastern end of the parish is part of the built-up area of Maidstone, although the remainder is much more rural. The River Medway is the southern boundary of the parish.

Barming is mentioned in the Domesday Book, and was then described as being divided into East and West; the latter being known as Little Barming, and having its own church until the 16th century.

Locally, the belief is that Barming is derived from the Victorian era Asylum that has since been demolished. However, that is not the case; one possible source gives the meaning as the yeast formed on malt liquors while fermenting. The origins come from the Old English *beorma*, or the Frisian *berme* – thus of Anglo-Saxon origins. The other origin, and more likely, is pre-Anglo-Saxon – *bearm-leath-ingas* or the *dwellers at the outlying woodland clearing*.

When George was managing his Croydon shop customers frequently asked for him by name – and thus the term asking for *Batts from Barming* became the well-known phrase.

George delighted in the term and at one time thought he should call his house *The Belfry* – Eileen, his wife, was less amused at the thought!

Foreword

I first met George on a visit to Normandy with a group of veterans in June 2016. He looked at me and said "That's not a proper tie, here, wear this" handing me a Normandy Veterans' Association tie which I have worn with pride ever since. I liked George immediately. I liked the no nonsense approach, the can-do spirit and the attention to detail that I saw in him and thought to myself, Grandfather would have approved.

It was this spirit that was vital to the success of D-Day. Thanks to the courage and determination of people like George and his comrades, many of whom gave the ultimate sacrifice, peace became a reality for the occupied peoples of Europe. Thankfully some, like George, are still with us to tell their stories.

It is that same spirit that has been the inspiration behind the efforts of the Normandy Memorial Trust to turn George's dream into reality. That dream was to build a lasting memorial behind Gold beach, where George landed on 6th June 1944, to honour in one place, all the 22,442 service men and women under British command who died in the Normandy campaign.

This memorial is long overdue and much needed. Needed by the families of those who died on the beaches and fields on Normandy; needed by the veterans so that they know that they and their comrades will never be forgotten; and needed by all of us who have been fortunate to have known 75 years of peace but need to be reminded of the cost at which that peace was bought. I look forward to reading George's story and I am very grateful to him for his passion and his vision – an example to us all.

Henry Montgomery

April 2019

George with the Hon. Henry Montgomery and the Rt. Hon. Lord Llewellyn of Steep, OBE PC.

Gold Beach; looking westwards, above, looking eastwards, below.

Foreword by Her Majesty's Ambassador to France, the Rt Hon Lord Llewellyn of Steep OBE PC

I first met George Batts in Normandy, during the commemorations for the 70th anniversary of D-Day in 2014.

I was captivated as George recounted to me what it was like, as an 18 year old Sapper in the Royal Engineers, landing among the first waves of British troops on Gold Beach – tasked with clearing the beach of mines and booby traps.

George told me too of his dream – indeed his determination - to see a Memorial built in Normandy to record the names, including so many of his mates, who lost their lives on D-Day and during the battle of Normandy which followed. The Americans have a memorial at Omaha beach, and the Canadians at Juno – but until now, remarkably, there has been no British equivalent.

Now, thanks to the efforts of George and his fellow Veterans, such a Memorial is being built, pioneered by the Normandy Memorial Trust, funded by the British Government and by many individual donations. It will be at Ver-sur-Mer, on a magnificent site overlooking Gold Beach, and with the famous Mulberry Harbour visible in the distance.

The Memorial will commemorate in perpetuity over 22,000 service personnel – British and those of our Allies - who lost their lives fighting under British command during the landings and the ensuing Normandy campaign.

The sculpture which will be at the heart of the Memorial is to unveiled during the commemorations to mark the 75th anniversary of D-Day, in the presence of the British Prime Minister and the President of France.

I hope that for George and his fellow Veterans, so many of whom make the journey to Normandy each year in defiance of their advancing age, this Memorial will show that their heroism, and the heroism of their comrades who made the ultimate sacrifice, will never be forgotten.

This book tells George's remarkable story. D-Day, and the campaign that followed it, were made up of thousands of similar stories of bravery and of sacrifice. We who come after know that it is to George and to his comrades that we owe our freedom.

We must never forget it, never take it for granted, never fail to defend what they won for us all those years ago – and at such a price.

Edward Llewellyn

May 2019

Index

Gold Beach, foot prints

Looking over my life for the past 93 years, has, as you may well imagine, been enlightening.

I started life as the offspring of loving parents and a younger brother. With Dad being in private service we never had much money – I have learned over the years that money is not everything – but we had a good house to live in. It also meant we were always living way out in the country and the advantage of a big estate in which to roam around and play. Although we had to make our own amusements and games we were never bored and became very adept in providing and inventing our own pastimes.

There is always criticism of the "gentry", their aloofness and treatment of the people - usually from those who have never experienced their parents working for them of living on the estates. But I have always found them, to be thoughtful towards their staff and their families and in the small villages in which I lived supplied sports' facilities for football, cricket and tennis etc. – for our use. These were always up to the highest standard.

We earned pocket money by working in the hay and harvest fields, picking fruit and all the other country pursuits. The comradeship and enjoyment at these times was unbelievable. It has to be admitted that times were hard, but we never knew any better and this never expected the earth. I can honestly say that we were contented with our lot and any small benefits was more than appreciated.

Although life was good, we were always encouraged to work hard at school and thus obtain a good education as it was recognised that this would ensure our lot in life would be enhanced. If we achieved these things, we were proud and therefore made the best of it, but as I said, we never expected the earth and therefore were satisfied with small mercies. Anything we achieved in life we had worked hard for, had earned and accepted.

Unfortunately, in September 1939, our idyllic life was interrupted and changed overnight by the declaration of war on Germany. For the next six to seven years we had a new learning curve. I do not believe that our life has ever been the same since then.

Although at the time I was only 14 years old, the voice of Neville Chamberlain, the Prime Minister, on the radio and the reaction at home, still so vivid in my memory. I could show you exactly where my Dad, Mum, sister and myself were sitting and the reaction from us all. Mum just went quiet; Dad, who had been in the trenches in the 1st World War, said God help us all and I had visions of life being difficult and the good days over..............

I would like to thank all my friends, especially those who have contributed to the book and the students of the History Society, St John's School [Gravesend] who carried out much research and furnished me with news of my family and background! ....A sincere thank you to all.

Chapter 1 - Family

George Robert Batts was born on August 21st, 1925 in Harefield, Middlesex at the home of his mother's parents. His parents were Mary Elizabeth Wiggins and George William [known as William] Batts. There were two children in the family – George had an older sister Marian Elsie who was born in 1922.

George was well aware that he shared a birthday date with Princess Margaret, later the Countess of Snowdon, CI, GCVO, GCStJ. Margaret Rose [1930 – 2002) was the younger daughter of King George VI and Queen Elizabeth and the only sibling of Queen Elizabeth II. Flags were flown on her birthday – August 21st – and George, when a young child was always delighted to note how the Country and specifically the Government honoured him on his birthday [he not realising the flags were not specifically for him!].

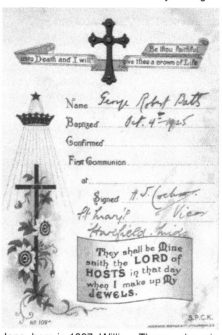

He was baptised on October 4th at St Mary's, Harefield.

William's parents were Robert Constantine and Mary Jane [Baden] Batts. Robert was born in 1856 in Bampton, Oxfordshire. He was a farm labourer. Mary Jane was born in 1857 in Swindon, Wiltshire. The couple married on February 23rd, 1878 at the Parish Church in Bampton, Oxfordshire. They had ten children – Robert Charles Fred, born in 1878, Francis James Barden, born in 1879, Robert Constantine, born in 1882, Elizabeth Amelia, born in 1885, Elsie Sarah, born in 1887. Beatrice May, born in 1893, George William, Florence Jane, born in 1897, William Thomas, born in 1899, John Henry, born in 1901 [died in 1902]. The family home was Queen Street, Bampton.

Robert died on February 19th, 1927. Probate on July 8th in London was to Robert Constantine [son - listed as a non-commissioned Officer in HM Army] and James Sparkes, [husband of Elsie] plasterer. The effects came to £663 12 shillings and 4 pence.

William was born on March 9th, 1895. He died in Northamptonshire in 1987.
William was employed in the [domestic] service sector rising to being butler in some of the great Houses of the country. The family came from Bampton, Oxfordshire. Bampton, also called Bampton-in-the-Bush, is a settlement and civil parish in the Thames Valley about 4½ miles southwest of Witney in Oxfordshire. The parish includes the hamlet of Weald. The 2011 Census recorded the parish's population as 2,564. Bampton has a tradition of Morris dancing which may be 600 years old.

Documentary and circumstantial evidence show that Morris dancing in Bampton goes back at least to the 1790s. It used to be performed in Bampton on Whit Monday but the date has recently changed to the late May Bank Holiday. The town is also the home of Bampton Classical Opera which performs both in Bampton and elsewhere. In Bampton the venue is the garden of the Deanery, a private house near St Mary's church.

The Society for the Preservation of Ancient Junketing (Spajers) organises the Bampton Shirt Race around the village on the late May Bank Holiday each year, celebrating the 14 pubs that used to be open. Runners, originally dressed in night-gowns in pairs, with one pushing another in a trolley, stop at the houses that are or were pubs and drink a measure of beer before running to the next.

Bampton is one of the settings for the fictional crime novels The Chronicles of Hugh de Singleton, set in about 1366, by Mel Starr. ITV used Bampton for several outdoor locations for the fictional village of Downton, North Yorkshire in the period drama television series *Downton Abbey*. The main ones included the Old Rectory (Churchgate House), the public library, the parish church of St Mary the Virgin, and houses in Church View that were used to represent two pubs

Bampton is variously referred to as both a town and a village. The Domesday Book recorded that it was a market town by 1086. It continued as such until the 1890s. It has both a town hall and a village hall.

George's mother Mary Elizabeth Wiggins came from Harefield, Middlesex. She was born on February 5th, 1902.

Mother and son shortly after George's birth in August 1925.

Mary's parents were Robert and Sarah Wiggins. Robert was born in 1870 in Southall, Middlesex. He worked locally in a brickworks. He created a fire proof brick which, as he did not patent himself, the brickworks benefitted from. He died in the 1920 when just 52 just after being promoted to manage a brickworks in Ireland. Sarah was born in 1867 in Harefield, Middlesex. The couple married in 1890 and had nine children – Sarah, born in 1890, Caroline, born in 1894, Marian May, born in 1896, Robert, born in 1899, Mary, John, born in 1904, Irene, born in 1907 and Percy Reginald, born in 1909. The family home was 16 Waterloo Villas, High Street, Harefield.

Harefield is a village in the London Borough of Hillingdon, England, on a hill, 17 miles northwest of Charing Cross near Greater London's boundary with Buckinghamshire to the west and Hertfordshire to the north. To the immediate west of Harefield was Coles Shadbolt Works. The site was originally developed for brickworks. Coles Shadbolt made Roman Cement on the Regent's Canal in Islington, and a dock on the Grand Union Canal was constructed at Harefield to ship bricks to Islington. In charge of this, Percy Shadbolt, who had previously worked at Waldringfield, recognised the suitability of the site for Portland cement. The plant was completed with twelve chamber kilns in 1880. However, the kilns were clearly installed piecemeal and over the years.

As with other plants, trials with slurry sprays were mandated in the late 1920s, and at the Blue Circle annual production conference, the plant manager gave a plaintive description of the resulting dust complaints from the well-heeled residents of the village. The plant's closure corresponded with major new kilns coming on line at Swanscombe. The plant never had a rail link, and used the canal for heavy freight. After clinker manufacture ceased, lime was made, using the rotary kiln, until the early 1940s, after which the site was completely cleared. Nothing remains visible: even the canal spur has disappeared.

William started his working life in 1910 at the age of 14 as a Hall Boy at Althorp House, Northamptonshire. Althorp is a Grade I listed stately home and estate, of about 13,000

William, second from right, at Althorp.

13

acres. It has been held by the prominent aristocratic Spencer family for more than 500 years, and has been owned by Charles Spencer, 9th Earl Spencer since 1992. It was also the home of Lady Diana Spencer (later Princess of Wales) from her parents' divorce until her marriage to Charles, Prince of Wales.

Althorp is mentioned as a small hamlet in the Domesday Book as "Olletorp", and by 1377 it had become a village with a population of more than fifty people. By 1505 there were no longer any tenants living there, and in 1508, John Spencer purchased Althorp estate with the funds generated from his family's sheep-rearing business. Althorp became one of the prominent stately homes in England. The mansion dates to 1688, replacing an earlier house that was once visited by Charles I. The Spencer family amassed an extensive art collection and other valuable household items. During the 18th century, the house became a major cultural hub in England, and parties were regularly held, attracting many prominent members of Great Britain's ruling class. George John, 2nd Earl Spencer, who owned Althorp between 1783 and his death in 1834, developed one of the largest private libraries in Europe at the house, which grew to over 100,000 books by the 1830s. After falling on hard times, John Spencer, 5th Earl Spencer, in 1892 sold much of the collection to Enriqueta Rylands, who was building the University of Manchester Library.

John Spencer, 5th Earl Spencer, known as the Red Earl, inherited Althorp in 1857. He served as a Liberal Party politician and was a close friend of the Prime Minister William Gladstone, who he served under in all four of his cabinets. After dying childless in 1910, John passed Althorp to his half brother, Charles Spencer, 6th Earl Spencer, who served as Lord Chamberlain from 1905 to 1912 in the Liberal administrations headed by Sir Henry Campbell-Bannerman and H. H. Asquith.

Leaving Althorp, William secured a position as footman at Hever Castle. Hever in Kent, near Edenbridge, 30 miles south-east of London, began as a country house, built in the 13th century. From 1462 to 1539, it was the seat of the Boleyn family. Anne Boleyn,spent her early youth there after her father, Thomas Boleyn, inherited it in 1505. The castle passed to him upon the death of his father, Sir William Boleyn.

There have been three main periods in the construction of this historic castle. The oldest part of the castle dates to 1270 and consisted of the gatehouse and a walled bailey. The second period was when the castle, then in need of repair, was converted into a manor in 1462 by Geoffrey Boleyn, younger brother of Thomas Boleyn, Master of Gonville Hall, Cambridge. He added a Tudor dwelling within the walls. The third period of repair and renovation was in the 20th century, when it was acquired by William Waldorf Astor. The property came into the possession of Henry VIII after the death of Anne's father, Thomas Boleyn, in 1539. He bestowed it upon Anne of Cleves in 1540 as part of the settlement following the annulment of their marriage. The Castle subsequently passed through various owners, including the Waldegrave family to 1715, the Humfreys family to 1749 and the Meade Waldo family to 1903.

In 1903, it was acquired and restored by the American millionaire William Waldorf Astor, who used it as a family residence. William Waldorf "Willy" Astor, 1st Viscount Astor (1848 – 1919), was a wealthy American-born attorney, politician, businessman, and newspaper publisher. He moved with his family to England in 1891, became a British subject in 1899, and was made a peer as Baron Astor in 1916 and Viscount Astor in 1917 for his contributions to war charities. He was a prominent member of the Astor family.

John Spencer, 5th Earl Spencer
Althorp House

William Waldorf Astor
Hever Castle

William enlisted at Buckingham Gate on March 13th, 1915 with the Grenadier Guards, service number 23661. He was 5 feet 10¼ inches tall, weighed 154 lbs with a girth of 39 inches. His records indicate that he had a *mole centre left cheek*, another *below right extremity of mouth* and another *below left extremity of mouth*! He was of good physical development.

The Grenadier Guards trace their lineage back to 1656, when Lord Wentworth's Regiment was raised in Bruges, in the Spanish Netherlands (present-day Belgium), from gentlemen of the Honourable Artillery Company by the then heir to the throne, Prince Charles (later King Charles II) where it formed a part of exiled King's bodyguard. A few years later, a similar regiment known as John Russell's Regiment of Guards was formed. In 1665, these two regiments were combined to form the 1st Regiment of Foot Guards, consisting of 24 companies of men. Since then the Grenadier Guards have served ten Kings and four Queens, including the current Queen Elizabeth II. Throughout the 18th century, the regiment took part in a number of campaigns including the War of Spanish Succession, the War of Austrian Succession and the Seven Years' War. At the end of the Napoleonic Wars, the regiment gained the name "Grenadier" in July 1815 following a Royal Proclamation.

Grenadier Guards

1 Reserve Battalion, private, guard order, England, 1918

2 Bandsman, full dress, 1914

3 2nd Battalion, sergeant, walking out dress, France, 1917

4 Officer, guard order, England

5 4th Battalion, private, marching order, France, 1917

A. E. Haswell Miller 1919

At the outbreak of the First World War in August 1914, the regiment consisted of three battalions. With the commencement of hostilities, the regiment raised a service battalion, the 4th Battalion, and a reserve battalion, known as the 5th (Reserve) Battalion, which was used to carry out ceremonial duties in London and Windsor during the war. The 2nd Battalion of the regiment was sent to France in August, and the 1st Battalion followed to Belgium in October. They took part in the early stages of the fighting during the period known as "Race to the Sea", during which time they were involved significantly at the First Battle of Ypres.

In February 1915, a fifth Guards regiment was raised, known as The Welsh Guards. In recognition of the significant contribution Welshmen had made to The Grenadier Guards, the regiment transferred five officers and 634 other ranks to the newly formed unit. A short time later, permission was received for the formation of the Guards Division, the brainchild of Lord Kitchener, and on August 18th, 1915, the division came into existence, consisting of three brigades, each with four battalions. Following this the four service battalions of the regiment fought in a number of significant battles including Loos, the Somme, Cambrai, Arras and the Hindenburg Line.

Following the Armistice with Germany in November 1918, the regiment returned to just three battalions, which were used in a variety of roles, serving at home in the United Kingdom, as well as in France, Turkey and Egypt.

William was admitted to hospital at Caterham with colic on June 29th, 1915, being discharged on July 10th. William left for the Front on July 16th, 1916 and joined the 1st Battalion. On the 27th he joined the 1st *in the field* and was assigned as *servant to Captain W D Drury-Lowe*, DSO, pictured. Captain Drury-Lowe would rise to the rank of Lieutenant Colonel with the 1st Battalion. He was born in London in 1877 and killed in action on September 25th, 1916, He is buried in Guards Cemetery, Lesbouef. He was the son of William Drury-Lowe and Lady Lucy Drury-Lowe and husband of the

Hon. Hylda Harriet Sugden, daughter of Edward Burtenshaw Sugden, 2nd Baron St. Leonards and Emma Sophia Dashwood, the marriage being in 1902.

In February 1900 he was commissioned as a 2nd Lieutenant in the Grenadier Guards. He served with the 3rd Battalion in South Africa from 1901-1902 and was decorated with the D.S.O. He succeeded his father to the Denby and Locko estates in 1906, and in July 1908 resigned from the army at the rank of Captain.

William was a J.P. for Derbyshire from 1907 and a Derbyshire County Councillor in 1913-1914. On the outbreak of the First World War William became a Captain in the Reserve of Officers.

In the same engagement where Drury-Lowe was killed William was wounded in the shoulder and both thighs – *gunshot wounds*. The machine gun spatters bullets quickly and indiscriminately. He was sent back to Dieppe and onto England to East Leeds Hospital to recover from his wounds and returned to the Front on October 20th. William was now transferred to the 2nd Battalion.

On April 19th, 1918 William was admitted to 4th Field Ambulance having taken ill - *hernia*. He was sent to 12th General Hospital, Rouen and onto 40th Stationary Hospital, Harfleur. From there he was sent for final recuperation to Le Havre. There he forfeited *5 days pay for breaking out of camp* on August 22nd and for *breaking back into camp*! On August 29th he re-joined the 2nd Battalion in the Field. He was granted leave to England on October 25th and re-joined the 2nd on November 22nd.

William was discharged on demobilisation on March 31st, 1920.

Post-War William continued in service; In 1931 he was Butler to Lord Manton - Miles Watson, 2nd Baron Manton (1899–1968), of Compton Verney, Warwickshire and Plumpton Place, East Sussex. He was the eldest son of Joseph Watson, 1st Baron Manton (1873–1922), the Leeds soap magnate, by his wife (Frances) Claire Nickols, daughter of Harold Nickols of Sandford House, Kirkstall, Leeds. Watson had three younger brothers, Robert Fraser, Alastair Joseph, and Richard Mark Watson, all born by 1906. He was educated at Harrow.

He succeeded as 2nd Baron Manton on the death of his father in 1922. He sold the Compton Verney estate to Samuel Lamb. In 1927, he sold the Manton racehorse training establishment near Marlborough, Wiltshire, which had been purchased by his father.

Miles Watson, 2nd Baron Manton (right) with brother R F Watson, Directors of Newmarket Bloodstock Ltd. Company Christmas card portrait circa 1960

In the 1920s Manton had been a jockey under National Hunt Rules. having sold his father's briefly-owned seat of Compton Verney. In 1938 he purchased Plumpton Place near Lewes in Sussex, where he established a racehorse stud. Hard Sauce, produced there, sired the winner of the 1958 Derby, Hard Ridden. For the British Bloodstock Agency, he travelled to India and South America. With his brother Robert he was a director of Newmarket Bloodstock Ltd.

He married twice - firstly in April 1923, to Alathea Alys Mary Pauline Langdale, 2nd daughter and co-heiress of Colonel Philip Joseph Langdale, OBE, JP, DL, of Houghton Hall, Sancton, Yorkshire. Alathea filed for divorce in 1934, which was granted in 1936. Secondly in June 1938, he married Leila Joan Reynolds daughter of Major Philip Guy Reynolds, DSO and formerly the wife of John Dane Player (1864-1950), a director of

John Player & Sons tobacco manufacturers founded by his father and of Imperial Tobacco, who had cited Manton in his own divorce proceedings, starting 1937. She became after Manton's death Lady Brownlow, having married, as his 3rd wife, Peregrine Cust, 6th Baron Brownlow of Belton House, Grantham, Lincolnshire. Manton died in June 1968 at his home Plumpton Place.

Compton Verney House is an 18th century country mansion at Compton Verney near Kineton in Warwickshire, England, which has been converted to house the Compton Verney Art Gallery. The building is a Grade I listed house built in 1714 by Richard Verney, 11th Baron Willoughby de Broke. It was first extensively extended by George Verney, 12th Baron Willoughby de Broke in the early 18th century and then remodelled and the interiors redesigned by Robert Adam for John Verney, the 14th Baron, in the 1760s. It is set in more than 120 acres of parkland landscaped by Lancelot "Capability" Brown in 1769.

The house and its 5,079-acre estate was sold by Richard Greville Verney, the 19th Baron, in 1921 to soap magnate Joseph Watson who was elevated to the peerage as *1st Baron Manton of Compton Verney* only two months before his death in March 1922 from a heart attack whilst out hunting with the Warwickshire Foxhounds at nearby Upper Quinton. George Miles Watson, 2nd Baron Manton sold the property to Samuel Lamb. It was requisitioned by the Army during World War II and became vacant when the war ended.

From Compton it was now onto Leckford in Hampshire and specifically to Leckford Abbess, the home of Spedan Lewis [*John Lewis*]. William worked here from 1931 until 1933. Leckford lies on the eastern bank of the River Test just to the south of its confluence with the River Anton, to the east of Longstock and south of Chilbolton. The parish has a population of around 136. The parish church, St Nicholas's has a 13th-century core, rebuilt in the 16th century and much restored since. Leckford was on the Andover Canal, which later became the Andover and Redbridge Railway, but did not have a station. In World War 2, Leckford shared a boundary with Chilbolton Aerodrome, which was used by the Allied air forces in the later days of World War II.

Spedan Lewis and Leckford Abbess.

The parish contains the Leckford Estate, owned by the John Lewis Partnership. Leckford Estate was purchased as a private estate by John Spedan Lewis of Oxford Street in 1929; a visionary retailer with an extensive knowledge of botany, entomology and aquatic life and the founder of the John Lewis Partnership.

Spedan invested heavily during his lifetime on the estate, particularly in housing, farming mechanisation, Partner welfare and the environment. There was even room for cricket – with the Oval used as the model! The Estate stands as a legacy to Spedan Lewis' devotion to experimentation, Partner happiness and the natural environment.

Spedan Lewis brought Leckford Estate in 1929. The original estate was c.1800 acres and Spedan's home was Leckford Abbess, which later became known as Leckford Abbas. Improvement were carried out on the Estate in the 1930s, this included the development of sustainable farming operations. A Bird Farm was established and the first copy of the Leckford Gazette was published. The first Leckford camp was introduced in 1937 (a facility for Retail working Partners to holiday). This holiday provision remains on the estate even today.

In the mid 40's the estate expanded into Longstock taking the entire estate to around 4,000 acres. Spedan Lewis moved from Leckford to Longstock House and spent much of his time improving the Water Gardens. The farm continued to produce food for the Waitrose shops and a substantial part of the Leckford side of the estate was commandeered as an airfield for the War effort. In 1955 Spedan Lewis retired and moved into a small house on the Estate. The farm continues to develop the types of produce grown on the estate. The Leckford Estate becomes part of the Waitrose trading division and officially the Waitrose Farm.

George displaying some ability with the bat at Leckford and, below, celebrating the Silver Jubilee Celebrations, May 1935, Gillingham, Dorset – George's sister Marian pushing the 'Jubilee Babies' 'pram and George, right, disguised as a fireman.

In 1933 William secured employment with Sir Harold Pelly in Gillingham, Dorset. He was born in February 1863, son of Sir John Henry Pelly 2nd Bart and Blanche Elizabeth Vincent daughter of Sir Frederick Vincent 11th Bt. He married Annie Montagu Poore, second daughter of Major Robert Poore of Old Lodge, Salisbury, Wiltshire in 1889. Robert Montagu Poore, DSO, CIE (1866 – 1938) was a Dublin born cricketer and army officer who, whilst serving in South Africa in 1896, played in three Tests for the South African cricket team. Much of his cricket was played when he held the rank of Major, but he eventually became a Brigadier-General. *Of all the people in the history of the game,* wrote Leo Cooper in an introduction to A. A. Thomson's *Odd Men In, he seems to stand for the Eccentric Ideal.*

Sir Harold was J.P. for Dorset & Wiltshire and was a leading figure in the Primrose League. The League was an organisation for spreading Conservative principles in Great Britain. It was founded in 1883. The family home was Thorngrove House, Common Mead Lane, Gillingham, Dorset and later (sometime pre-1942) at Lytchett Hard, Upton, Poole, Dorset. He died in November 1950. Sir Harold's eldest daughter Benita Blanche married Alan Francis [Brooke], later 1st Viscount Alanbrooke, KG GCB GCVO OM in December 1929. She was previously married to Sir Thomas Evans Keith Lees, 2nd Bart., of South Lytchet, Dorset.

George thoroughly enjoyed himself in Gillingham. He was a member of the Church Choir and was also a Scout – the troop being attached to the Choir. George enjoyed the work with the choir, the singing, the concerts, the camping and the jamborees.

A Unionist and Primrose League Gathering at Thorngrove, July 23rd, 1908. Those pictured include Mr. H. Syndercombe Bower; Viscount Midleton P.C., Lady Pelly [seated second from left], Sir Harold Pelly [seated front centre and wearing a Primrose league badge), Mrs. Alfred Morrison [seated second from right] and Sir Elliot Lees, Bart.

In 1936 William moved to Sussex and the employment of Mr John Hornung at his estate, West Grinstead Park. The House was demolished in the 1960s.

Members of the Hornung family gathered at West Grinstead Park to celebrate Pitt and Laura Hornung's 50th wedding anniversary, April 1934.

John Peter 'Pitt' Hornung was an entrepreneur who founded a number of sugar cane plantations in Portuguese East Africa (later Mozambique), known as the Sena Sugar Estates, in the late nineteenth and twentieth centuries; he was also a breeder of race horses, establishing the West Grinstead Stud in the 1920s.

Pitt Hornung was born in 1861 in Cleveland Hills, Middlesbrough, England; his parents were immigrants from Transylvania who set up a flourishing trade and shipping business in the area. After being educated at the Collegiate School in Edinburgh, Scotland, he was sent away by his parents to work on a ranch in Uruguay. Upon his return to England, Pitt was again sent overseas to work, this time in Lisbon, Portugal. In 1883, Pitt met and married Laura de Paiva Raposo, whose father held a number of concessions, or *prazos*, along the Zambezi delta in Portuguese East Africa. After the death of both his father and father-in-law, Pitt turned his own attentions to the concessions and, in 1889, he decided to attempt to establish sugar cane plantations at the concessions in Mopeia.

Despite a number of setbacks, the first sugar was cut at Mopeia in 1893, producing a modest 600 tons. Nonetheless, the venture was successful enough to enable Pitt to raise sufficient funds to establish a second plantation and factory at nearby Caia, in 1906; the resulting company was known as the Sena Sugar Factory. By buying out other, less successful sugar cane concessions which had sprung up in the region and transforming them into successful entities – including a concession at Marromeu - Pitt's business went from strength to strength, and he established a sugar cane empire. The various concerns were grouped into one company – the Sena Sugar Estates – in 1920, and a further factory was established at Luabo in 1922.

As a result of his activities in Portuguese East Africa, Pitt became a wealthy man. Seeking a gentile lifestyle back in England, Pitt moved his family from Strawberry Hill in Twickenham, near London, to West Grinstead Park, West Sussex, which he purchased in 1913 from Sir Merrick Burrell. Having acquired a passion for both the breeding and racing of horses, Pitt eventually established his own stud, registering the West Grinstead Stud in 1924. Pitt enjoyed some considerable success as a breeder, and the West Grinstead Stud produced 129 winners over 26 years.

Pitt Hornung died in February 1940. West Grinstead Park was sold off and the stud went on to become part of the National Stud in 1949, although one of Pitt's sons, Colonel Charles Hornung, went on to establish his own stud in Cowfold, West Sussex, in 1950. The Sena Sugar Estates remained a family concern until 1986, when the estates were sacked by Mozambique's Renamo rebels during the country's civil war.

William feeding the deer at West Grinstead Park, late 1930s.

William and Mary are recorded on the National Register [for identity card issue] as living at West Grinstead Park with William recorded as being a butler. He is also recorded as being a Reserve Special Constable. The War reserve constable was a voluntary role within the ranks of the British police forces. As suggested by the title, the role was as a voluntary police constable during the war. War reserve constables were sworn in under the Special Constables Act 1923, and had the full powers of a police officer.

The War Reserve Police was introduced in 1939 and at the height of World War II in 1944 there were 17,000 war reserve constables. The rank was dissolved on December 31st 1948, causing 686 officers to be discharged from service, and the remainder being recruited for service as a regular or special constable.

Despite British police traditionally being unarmed, during the war officers were armed with Canadian Ross rifles for protection from enemy action, enemy sabotage and to assist with the armed forces. Duties of a WRC included the usual activities of a constable, as well as enforcing blackouts, combating black market activity, assisting in evacuations and air raids, and capturing deserting soldiers.

Uniform and equipment was the same as a regular constable, with the exception of uniform epaulettes which were detailed WRC above the collar number and divisional sign. During the war officers wore named Brodie helmets instead of traditional police headgear.

The National Registration Act 1939 was an Act of Parliament in the United Kingdom introducing identity cards. The initial National Registration Bill was introduced to Parliament as an emergency measure at the start of World War II. Royal assent given on September 5th, 1939. The Act established a National Register which began operating on September 29th, 1939 (National Registration Day), a system of identity cards, and a requirement that they must be produced on demand or presented to a police station within 48 hours. On February 21st, 1952, it no longer became necessary to carry an identity card. The National Registration Act of 1939 was repealed on May 22nd, 1952.

William also served in World War 2 – being a sergeant with the South Harting, Petersfield [Hampshire] Home Guard. The unit was base at Uppark. The house, set high on the South Downs, was built for Ford Grey (1655—1701), the first Earl of Tankerville, *circa* 1690, the architect is believed to have been William Talman. The estate was sold in 1747 to Sir Matthew Fetherstonhaugh and his wife Sarah. Matthew and Sarah redecorated the house extensively from 1750 to 1760 and introduced most of the existing collection of household items displayed today, much of it collected on their Grand Tour of 1749 to 1751. Their only son, Sir Harry Fetherstonhaugh, added to the collection and commissioned Humphry Repton to add a new pillared portico, dairy and landscaped garden. In the 19th century stables and kitchens were added as separate buildings, connected to the main building by tunnels. Sir Harry famously married at the age of 71 the estate's dairy maid, 21-year-old Mary Ann Bullock, to whom he left Uppark on his death in 1846. She in turn, after considerably upgrading the property, left it to her sister Frances on her own death in 1874. Frances bequeathed it in 1895 to Lt. Col. The Hon. Keith Turnour, who assumed the name Fetherstonhaugh and lived there for 35 years, eventually leaving the estate to a friend's son, the future Admiral Sir Herbert Meade, who also adopted the Fetherstonhaugh name.

Herbert Meade was the third son of Richard Meade, 4th Earl of Clanwilliam, later Admiral of the Fleet, and Elizabeth Henrietta Kennedy. He adopted the additional surname of Fetherstonhaugh by Royal Licence in 1931. He joined the Royal Navy and was promoted Lieutenant in 1897, Commander in 1908 and Captain in 1914. In 1912 he was given command of HMS *Goshawk* which took part in the Battle of Heligoland in 1914 and was instrumental in the sinking of the German destroyer *V187*. He was put in command of the light cruisers HMS *Royalist* at the Battle of Jutland in 1916 and HMS *Ceres* at the Second Battle of Heligoland Bight in 1917.

From April 1918 to April 1919 he was the Naval Assistant to the Second Sea Lord and then took command for a short time of the battlecruiser HMS *Renown* before being appointed for three years as Captain of the Royal Naval College, Dartmouth (1923–26). In 1924 he was also appointed Naval Aide-de-Camp to the king. He was made a Commander of the Royal Victorian Order (CVO) in July 1922, a Companion of the Order of the Bath (CB) in the 1925 Birthday Honours and advanced to Knight Commander of the Royal Victorian Order (KCVO) in May, 1929. He was promoted to vice-Admiral on May 8th 1930 and in 1931 given the post of Vice-Admiral Commanding H.M. Yachts, a position he held until December 1934. He was promoted to the rank of admiral on July 31st 1934, advanced to Knight Grand Gross of the Royal Victorian Order (GCVO) in December of that year and retired at his own request in July 1936.

From 1939 to 1946 he was Sergeant-at-Arms of the House of Lords. He died in 1964.

William ensured that his unit was immaculately turned out – it would appear that the saying *once a Guardsman, always a Guardsman* was very much the case in this respect. Not alone did William expect a good turn out he also ensured that his unit maintained their shooting skills. The unit frequently attended competition at Bisley and participation had to be matched with success on the shooting range.

South Harting Home Guard, William is third from left, front row. The unit comprised various titled members. Photograph taken late Summer, 1940.

From Sussex it was onto Northampton, specifically Castle Ashby House, the home of William Bingham Compton. The 6th Marquess of Northampton, DSO (1885 – 1978) was the eldest son of William George Spencer Scott Compton, 5th Marquess of Northampton, and his wife Mary Florence (née Baring). He was educated at Eton College and Balliol College, Oxford, where he graduated as B.A. in 1906.

Initially a Lieutenant in the Northamptonshire Yeomanry, he was commissioned into the regular army in the Royal Horse Guards, of which he became Adjutant in 1913 and achieved the rank of Major. He fought in the First World War, during which he was twice mentioned in despatches and wounded. He was appointed a Commander of the Order of Leopold (Belgium) and in 1919 he was awarded the Distinguished Service Order. He was also a Commander of the Order of St John of Jerusalem. He transferred as a Captain to the Warwickshire Yeomanry in 1921 and rose to the rank of Lieutenant-Colonel in command, retiring in 1932. He was also Honorary Colonel of the 11th Battalion of the London Regiment (Finsbury Rifles) from 1923 to 1934.

He served in local government on the Northamptonshire County Council, to which he was elected in 1922, became Chairman in 1949, and resigned in 1955. He also became DL in 1936 for the Scottish County of Ross, and DL for Northamptonshire in 1937, as well as J.P. for the latter county.

As Earl Compton, he became engaged in 1912 to divorced actress Miss Daisy Markham (*alias* Mrs Annie Moss), who during the relationship ceased her acting work and bore him twin children. As result of family pressure he broke off the engagement after succeeding to his peerage, which led to a breach of promise lawsuit by Markham. She accepted from him a settlement of £50,000 (worth under £2,153,000 in 2005), a record in British legal history for a breach of promise case, in 1913.

William's completed his service with none other than the Duke of Buccleuch, Walter John Montagu Douglas Scott, the 8th Duke specifically at Boughton House in Northamptonshire.

The title Duke of Buccleuch, formerly also spelt Duke of Buccleugh, is a title created twice in the Peerage of Scotland. The second creation dates to April 1663. The Dukedom was for the Duke of Monmouth, who was the eldest illegitimate son of Charles II of Scotland, England, and Ireland, and who had married Anne Scott, 4th Countess of Buccleuch. The Duke also holds the Dukedom of Queensberry, created in 1684.

Anne Scott was created Duchess of Buccleuch in her own right along with her husband, James Scott, 1st Duke of Monmouth; thus, her title was unaffected by Monmouth's attainder of 1685. The title passed on to their descendants, who have successively borne the surnames Scott, Montagu-Scott, Montagu Douglas Scott and Scott again. In 1810, the 3rd Duke of Buccleuch inherited the Dukedom of Queensberry, also in the Peerage of Scotland, thus separating that title from the Marquessate of Queensberry. Thus, the holder is one of only five people in the UK to hold two or more different dukedoms, the others being the Duke of Cornwall and Rothesay, the Duke of Hamilton and Brandon, the Duke of Argyll (who holds two dukedoms named Argyll), and the Duke of Richmond, Lennox and Gordon.

The substantial origin of the ducal house of the Scotts of Buccleuch dates back to the large grants of lands in Scotland to Sir Walter Scott of Kirkurd and Buccleuch, a border chief, by James II, in consequence of the fall of William Douglas, 8th Earl of Douglas (1452), but the family traced their descent back to a Sir Richard le Scott (1240–1285). Sir Walter Scott of Branxholme and Buccleuch (died 1552) distinguished himself at the Battle of Pinkie Cleugh (1547). His great-grandson Sir Walter was created Lord Scott of Buccleuch in 1606. The family seats are Bowhill House, three miles outside Selkirk, representing the Scott line; Drumlanrig Castle in Dumfries and Galloway, representing the Douglas line; and Boughton House in Northamptonshire, representing the Montagu line.

Walter John Montagu Douglas Scott, 8th Duke of Buccleuch and 10th Duke of Queensberry, KT, GCVO, TD, PC (1894 – 1973) was a Scottish peer and Conservative politician. He was the son of John Montagu Douglas Scott, 7th Duke of Buccleuch and Lady Margaret Alice "Molly" Bridgeman. His sister, Alice, married Prince Henry, Duke of Gloucester (one of the paternal uncles of Queen Elizabeth II) in 1935, becoming a member of the Royal Family. Montagu Douglas Scott was educated at Eton and Christ Church, Oxford, and had a military career commanding the 4th KOSBs. He was also Captain-General of the Royal Company of Archers.

As Earl of Dalkeith, Scott was Scottish Unionist Party Member of Parliament (MP) for Roxburghshire and Selkirkshire from 1923 until 1935, when he succeeded as Duke of Buccleuch and Duke of Queensberry. He was succeeded as MP for the constituency by his brother, Lord William Scott. According to Cowling, he met German ambassador Joachim von Ribbentrop in London. Seen as pro-German, he was compelled to 'resign' as Lord Steward by King George VI.

William Bingham Compton,
The 6th Marquess of Northampton, DSO
Castle Ashby

Walter John Montagu Douglas Scott,
8th Duke of Buccleuch,
Broughton House

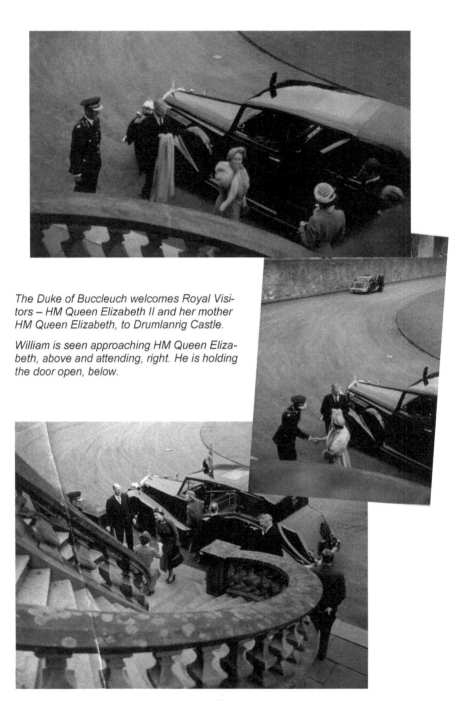

The Duke of Buccleuch welcomes Royal Visitors – HM Queen Elizabeth II and her mother HM Queen Elizabeth, to Drumlanrig Castle.

William is seen approaching HM Queen Elizabeth, above and attending, right. He is holding the door open, below.

William's two brothers also served in the Great War – Billy served with the Coldstream Guards and Bob served with the Irish Guards. Billy survived the war and returned to Bamford on the cessation of hostilities to continue being a farm labourer.

Bob was Mess Caterer with the 2nd Battalion, Irish Guards. He enlisted on December 12th, 1915 at Caterham Barracks at the age of 33 years and 122 days stating his occupation as that of a butler. He was 5 feet 9 inches tall, weighed 172lbs with a girth of 41 inches. He was described as being of good physical development. His next of kin is given as his wife Ida Palagie. They had married at Notre Dame de France Church at the Guards' Barracks on May 15th, 1913. Bob, service number 11309, was posted to 3rd Battalion on June 1st, 1916. He was promoted Corporal on January 27th, 1917 and Lance Sergeant on March 1st, 1917. He was appointed Sergeant January 11th, 1919. He relinquished his stripes on transfer to the 1st Battalion on March 1st, 1919. On August 28th, 1919 he volunteered for the Army of Occupation [of the Rhineland]. On September 15th he was granted 21 days leave with an additional 13 days added. He remained with the Army of Occupation until December 18th and was demobilised on April 2nd, 1920.

The Irish Guards regiment was formed on April 1st, 1900 by order of Queen Victoria to commemorate the Irishmen who fought in the Second Boer War for the British Empire. Following the outbreak of the First World War, 1st Battalion, The Irish Guards was deployed to France almost immediately, and they remained on the Western Front for the duration of the war. During the early part of the war, the battalion took part in the Battle of Mons and formed the Allied rearguard during the Great Retreat. The battalion then took part in one of the bloodiest battles of 1914, the First Battle of Ypres, which began on October 19th, which left major casualties among the old Regular Army.

The 1st Battalion was involved in fighting for the duration of 'First Ypres', at Langemarck, Gheluvelt and Nonne Bosschen. The 1st Battalion suffered huge casualties between November 1st – 8th holding the line against near defeat by German forces, while defending Klein Zillebeke.

In May 1915, the 1st Irish Guards took part in the Battle of Festubert, though did not see much action. Two further battalions were formed for the regiment in July. In September that year, the battalion, as well as the 2nd Irish Guards, who had reached France in August, took part in the Battle of Loos, which lasted from September 25th until early October. Both battalions spent the rest of 1915 in the trenches and did not fight in any major engagements.

This relative quiet period for the regiment was broken on July 11th, 1916 when the Battle of the Somme began. The 1st Irish Guards took part in an action at Flers–Courcelette where they suffered severe casualties in the attack in the face of withering fire from the German machine-guns. The battalion also took part in the action at Morval before they were relieved by the 2nd Irish Guards.

In 1917 the Irish Guards took part in the Battle of Pilkem which began on July 31st during the Third Battle of Ypres. The Irish Guards also took part in the Battle of Cambrai in that year, the first large use of the tank in battle took place during the engagement. In 1918 the regiment fought in a number of engagements during the Second Battle of the Somme, including at Arras and Albert. The regiment then went on to take part in a number of battles during the British offensives against the Hindenburg Line.

On November 11th, 1918 the Armistice with Germany was signed. The 1st Battalion, Irish Guards were at Maubeuge when the Armistice was signed. The regiment's continued existence was threatened briefly when Winston Churchill, who served as Secretary of State for War between 1919 and 1921, sought the elimination of the Irish Guards and Welsh Guards as an economy measure. This proposal, however, did not find favour in government or army circles and was dropped. Between the wars, the regiment was deployed at various times to Turkey, Gibraltar, Egypt and Palestine.

Bob was a career soldier and re-engaged with the Irish Guards until retirement. One memory George has of him was of a visit to the Tower of London where Bob was stationed with the 2nd Battalion. George distinctly remembers the Deveruex Tower and a dark patch in the ceiling; he was convinced that it was the blood of victims of the King's justice!

The Devereux Tower is situated in the north-west corner of the inner curtain wall and was built by King Henry III, an avid royal builder, between 1238 - 1272, when it was known as 'Robyn the Devil's' Tower The tower consists of two stories, with an apartment in each, joined by a spiral stone staircase. Secret passages once ran from the Devereux Tower to the Chapel of St.Peter ad Vincula and the Beauchamp Tower. Much of the tower was rebuilt from the mid eighteenth century.

The tower acquired its present name from its most famous prisoner, Robert Devereux, Earl of Essex (1565 - 1601) who was executed for treason on the command of Queen Elizabeth I.

George remembers his Uncle Bob wearing a naval cap when seeing him. Bob and his wife Ida moved to Southampton where he enjoyed the sport of yachting, hence the naval cap! Ida's family suffered during World War 2 when the area where they lived in Milan was bombed by Allied Forces,

Billy was born on May 8th, 1899. He served with the Coldstream Guards in the Great War, service number 344205. His wife Blanche was born on April 8th, 1899. They married in February 1928 and two months later on April 21st they were bound for Canada. They sailed on the *Majestic* from Southampton. They were bound for Toronto to take up the opportunity of owning their own farm. However they had returned to England by 1939 as they are registered as living in Witney, Oxfordshire not far from Bampton on the 1939 National Register; Billy's occupation is listed as stoker with the Air Ministry.

George's sister, Marian was born in 1922 in Bryanston Square, London. Bryanston Square is a long, rectangular, terraced square in Marylebone, Westminster, London, originally of 50 sequentially numbered houses. Her father William had employment in the Square with the family living in a Mews Flat. Marian died in 2015.

Marian trained as a hairdresser in Horsham from 1936 through to 1939. Her father paid for the apprenticeship which was the norm at the time and which came to £50 in total. Marian was paid the princely sum of 2 shillings and 6 pence a week in her first year. She received five shillings a week the following year and in her final year she was paid seven shillings and six pence. She secured a position in London but was conscripted in 1940.

Marian served with the Land Army, right, during World War 2 – a not surprising war time service bearing in mind the family background.

Marian – the Land Army Girl.

Marion on her wedding day with her parents – William and Mary, right and below, the two bridesmaids – one being George's daughter Linda.

Marian married Dennis Barrett in 1957. He was born in 1930 and was from Putney. He was the son of William Stanley Leslie and Amy Florence Barrett. William lost both legs in the Great War.

Dennis worked in the Travel Business, specifically with Thomas Cook. His career started with selling train tickets at Harrods he would eventually become Sales Manager with Thomas Cook. He died in 2012 at the age of 82.

Dennis' older brother flew with 107th Squadron, Royal Air Force. Sergeant [Observer] William John Barrett, D.F.M., service number 580566, was killed in action on June 23rd, 1940. It appears that he baled out of the aircraft and the parachute opened successfully. However, he was killed when hit by ground-fire. He is buried in Amsterdam New Eastern Cemetery. The D.F.M. was gazetted on February 20th, 1940 and was the first D.F.M. to be awarded in World War 2.

Flying out from RAF Wattisham, Suffolk at 1.35pm three Belnheims MkIVs were tasked to attack an airfield at Soest in the Netherlands. Because of the weather they decided to turn back and attack the alternative target at Schipol. The formation came under attack by Leutnant Michael Sonner flying a Bf109E from 3./JG-51. Sonner shot down two of the Blenheims – all three crew in Blenheim L8754 were killed including the pilot Flying Officer Thomas Clare Prescott who is buried in the same cemetery as William. Sonner himself was killed on April 4th, 1943 by which time he was an Ace with six 'kills'.

The second Blenheim, N3593, shot down was flown by Flight Lieutenant John William Stephens. He survived the encounter and was taken prisoner. After the war and now a Squadron Leader serving with 8 Squadron in Aden, he was killed flying a Buckmaster T1 when the aircraft struck the ground during an asymmetric overshoot on April 21st, 1952. The other two crew of N3593 were killed – William and Sergeant Peter Edward Frederick Adams. Adams was initially listed as missing, believed killed. In 1951 his body was found and he is buried in Jonkebos War Cemetery. The Blenheim itself crashed near the Anthony Fokkerweg, Amsterdam.

William John Barrett/Barratt – service record.

Chapter 2- Education

George's earlier education and choice of schools was dictated to an extent by where his father William was employed. George's first attended school in 1929 when just four years old. The school was in Compton. George's father was then in the employment of Baron Manton at Compton Verney.

The journey to school every morning [and the return journey home] involved a 3 – 4 mile walk. If nothing else George worked on his fitness and ensured a solid ground work for future sporting endeavours!

In 1931 the family moved to Leckbridge in Hampshire, William now being employed by John Spedan Lewis.

Spedan Lewis bought the estate – some 4,000 acres - in Leckford, near Stockbridge, Hampshire in 1929. Spedan Lewis joined his father's John Lewis department store on Oxford Street, London, in 1914. It was around this time that he first realised that the salaries of himself, his brother and his father were the same amount of money as the combined salaries of everyone employed by the John Lewis stores. In 1909, a serious horse-riding accident meant that he could not work for nearly two years. It was during this time that he seems to have first evolved the desire to share profits with his employees, and which grew over time in scope and detail to become the underpinnings of the John Lewis Trust and John Lewis Partnership.

Assuming control of the Oxford Street store with his father's death in 1928, Lewis officially formed the John Lewis Partnership, and began the distribution of profits among its employees in 1929. He completed the move towards employee-ownership in 1950, with the transfer of control to the employees. Spedan Lewis resigned as chairman in 1955.

George continued his primary education at the Primary School in Stockbridge [right] nearby.

The journey to school was now a mere mile and a half.

Leckford had a population of just over a hundred and virtually everyone was an employee of *John Lewis*, the farms and the estate. There was even a replica of the Oval [home of Surrey County Cricket Club] created for the villagers and George has memories of honing his skills in the nets and actually playing on the ground, there being several. Cricket teams using the ground as their base.

By a very strange coincidence it was here that George's father William spent time recovering at a convalescent home after being wounded at the Front in the Great War. That was in 1917.

After a two-year sojourn in Hampshire, the family moved to Dorset in 1933 for three glorious years as George remembers. This was where his father William was a butler to Sir Harold Pelly at Thorngrove House, Gillingham.

The journey to school was two miles but the means of transport had changed – George was now on a bicycle. The old Victorian building [right] is still intact and still standing in the village.

It was here that George began to show his all-round abilities – and it was not just at sport that George was excelling, he was now showing much promise with his voice and became an invaluable member of the Choir.

As well as becoming a member of the Church Choir George also became a Scout – the troop were in fact attached to the Choir, becoming a member of one meant being a member of the other. To become a member of the Choir every boy had to have their voice trained for the exact purpose of singing in tune and in harmony. This task fell to the very able Reverend J.H.A. Charles. He later went on to Canterbury Cathedral as a Precentor. Some years later, with the family in Horsham, the Reverend Charles called to see George's parents asking if he [George] would join the Choir at Canterbury Cathedral. Unfortunately, the fees at King's School, Canterbury was greater than the yearly income of George's father William.

The Church Choir in Gillingham were well known in the area and in the County and many well attended concerts were given. George remembers vividly being at the Annual Festival Concert at the Crystal Palace on June 20th, 1936. There were in excess of 4,000 voices that particular year. It was a phenomenal and quite unforgettable experience especially for George who was just ten years old.

The Annual Concert was organised by The Free Church Union. The Union had been founded in 1888. A history of the Union written in 1930 by James T Lightfoot wrote that it was *a large and representative association* which could *assist congregations in many ways by helping to organise choral festivals in large centres and by establishing a library of music.* Thus, the Association was formed and met for its first Festival at the Crystal Palace. In 1925, it took on the present name of the Free Church Choir Union and Festivals continued to take place. The FCCU has a splendid heritage and can well glory in its past when a large number of famous singers have sung with the choir.

The centenary of the founding was celebrated at Coventry Cathedral in 1988. This was not the 100th Festival, due to the years of the two World Wars when Festivals did not take place. The 1936 Festival was the last one with the Crystal Palace as the venue; the Palace was demolished by fire on November 30th that year.

The time at Gillingham was for George a wonderful experience. There was the Choir and the Scouts; there were the concerts, the camping and the Scout Jamborees. Without any of these there would have been no holidays and adventures for the participants.

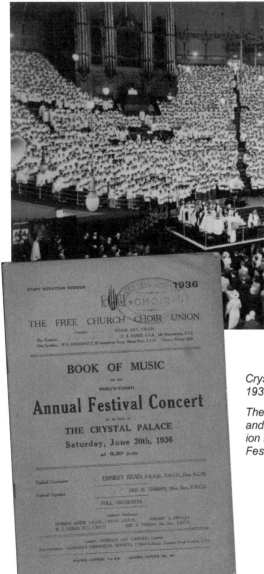

Crystal Palace, Saturday June 20th, 1936.

The 4,000 massed singers, above, and the Free Church Choir Union Book of Music for the Annual Festival Concert, right.

In 1936 William left the employment of John Spedan Lewis and secured a position at West Grinstead Park Sussex with Mr John Hornung. This move would have a major impact on George's life; not alone did he settle to secondary school for the next five years but he would also meet his future wife, Eileen in Horsham.

George was a pupil at Collyer's School, Horsham. He remained at the School for five years, from 1936 until 1941. The Headmaster at the time was Philip Tharp who had taken up the position in 1922 and would remain Headmaster until 1956. George regards his move to Collyer's as a real turning point in his life. However, he also feels that he never really settled in – there being several reasons for this.

George had moved from Dorset where life was certainly different. He was a scholarship pupil among the majority of fee-paying boys. There had also been a problem with the move from Dorset to Collyer's but this had been ironed out. George, of course, did not know anyone and new friends had to be made. In addition, there was the travel distance. There was the nine-mile journey by train – the station being closer to home – but the train times did not facilitate arriving in school on time. Thus, it was the bus. This meant a further mile and a half cycle to the bus stop. This meant leaving home at 7.30am and not being home until 5.45pm and there was homework to be done after that. With games the 5.45pm was extended by an hour or two.

The College of Richard Collyer, formerly called Collyer's School, is a co-educational sixth form college in Horsham, West Sussex, England. It is the second oldest school in West Sussex after The Prebendal School in Chichester and the fourth oldest school in Sussex. The college is Grade II listed by English Heritage.

The College was founded in 1532 (Old Style) in the will of Richard Collyer, who was born in Horsham, and became a wealthy member of The Mercers' Company of the City of London. The Mercers' Company are still the school's trustees, and maintain a close relationship with the school. Collyer willed that one of his houses in the City, variously called 'The Sonne' or 'The Sunne', be sold and the proceeds used to build a school-house in Horsham for "the number of thre score scholars". Under the terms of the will the money was not freed until 1540, and the new school was eventually opened in the early summer of 1541. The education granted to those sixty scholars, who were naturally all boys, was to be provided "freely without any money paying therefor", with the Mercer's Company paying the masters' salaries.

The original building was on the site of the current St Mary's Church of England Primary School, adjacent to the parish church. However, it was extended then rebuilt in 1660, in order to accommodate "neare an hundred scholars ... with diligence and good

Collyer's School, Horsham – then and now –
1930s, above and 2019, below.

success" by 1666, such that none of Collyer's original structure survives. (Part of the 1660 building remains in structure of Arun House, in Denne Road.) In the eighteenth century it fell into disrepair, such that the Mercers' Company surveyor reported that it would cost £1,040 to renovate, "but you will still have a very old and imperfect building." Accordingly, in 1840 the second building was demolished (save for the part incorporated into Arun House), and a new, late-Elizabethan style structure built for the sum of £2,240.

By the late nineteenth century, the population of Horsham had expanded to 10,000 (accelerated by the coming of the railway and its associated employment), the City and Guilds Institute (which the Mercers' Company had helped found) decreed that education needed to be extended to include the new sciences, and money needed to be found to replace the school buildings yet again. Thus after a long campaign against fees, including a petition of 1,100 signatures, the new school charter of 1889 stated that, "Tuition fees might vary between £4 and £10 p.a. and Boarding fees were not to exceed £40 a year." A new and larger site was sorely needed.

The present site in Hurst Road was found, and the current building was designed in 1892 by Arthur Vernon, and built by Joseph Potter for a contract price of £5,795. It is now grade II listed by English Heritage. Above the entrance is a stone engraved with, "Grammar School, Founded by Richard Collier AD 1532". (Historically the founder's name was often spelled as 'Collier', but from the twentieth century it has always been spelled as it is today.) The 1892 building facing Hurst Road has been extended continually as the school has expanded. This included the addition of science laboratories in 1897, a 'Great Hall' in 1912, and the 'New Block' classrooms in 1932.

In the 1890s Collyer's taught 110 boys from ages 7 to 17, both boarders and day-schoolers, and for the first time included a sixth form to study for university entrance. From 1923 the Rev. W.M. Peacock started to model the school on public school lines, introducing (among other things) four houses, *The Horsham Grammar School Magazine* (later to become *The Collyerian*), and a school song. By 1926 it was a single-stream school of 220 boys with a sixth form of "less than a dozen", and ten teaching staff.

Collyer's ceased to accept boarders in 1935, and the dormitories were converted into much-needed library and common-room space. Plans for adding a gymnasium and other facilities were abandoned in 1939, when the school accepted evacuees from the Mercers' School in London, and pupil numbers soared to over 400 in three streams. (The accommodation crisis was solved by building hutted classrooms, but numbers continued to rise because of the post-war 'baby boom', and the huts were not demolished until the 1980s.) In 1944 it became a voluntary-aided grammar school, and its education was again made available free to the scholars. In the 1950s it had around 500 pupils, rising slowly to over 600 during the 1960s.

In the early 1960s when an Old Collyerian (OC), Doctor William W. Duckering (1861–1945) bequeathed £22,000 to the school 'for its general purposes'. The bequest paid for a new laboratory block, gymnasium and changing rooms in 1961, and an assembly and dining hall with theatrical stage facilities, modern kitchens attached, and a 'Small Upper Hall' above the new foyer, all completed in 1963. The new hall was named the 'Duckering Hall', and the smaller hall the 'Duckering Room'. (The final phase of building work, to be a new classroom block replacing the World War Two emergency wooden huts, was never undertaken.) Between 1960 and 1963 the playing fields were also extended, levelled, and new sports facilities were added. In 1964 a headmaster's house was built on the site, replacing the accommodation that was originally included in the 1892 school block.

It started its transition to become a voluntary-aided sixth form college in 1976. The other three state secondary schools in Horsham (Forest Boys, Forest Girls and Horsham High School for Girls) became comprehensives. Collyer's had taken its last first form intake in the previous September, and started to expand its sixth form. Initially this was done by taking students from the two existing secondary moderns to do O-levels, and girls from Horsham High School who wanted to study A-level choices that were not offered by their previous school. There are currently 1,600 pupils at the College.

George's first experience of overseas travel came in the Summer of 1939 when he was still 13 years old. The trip to Europe was £8, a paltry sum now a days but quite a hefty amount eighty years ago. Not alone were the winds of war beginning to blow across Europe in August 1939 but Britain, France and Germany were on a war footing and everyone waited for the eventuality of war. However, if the tour had been paid for one should not therefore waste the money!

There were 15 students and 2 staff in the party which made its way to Newhaven for the ferry. The Channel Crossing to Dieppe was uneventful other than the mounting excitement that everyone was experiencing. There was a two day stop in Paris which was quite magical especially for those who had never been outside England before.

On the ferry, August 1939.

From Paris it was onto Zurich in Switzerland for another two-day sojourn. From there it was onto Lake Constance and a four day stop in the mountains nearby. George was highly impressed and somewhat horrified on a day trip to Friedrichshafen which lies just inside the border of Germany on the other side of Lake Garda from Switzerland. The encounter with members of the *Hitler Jugend* [Hitler Youth] and of the *Bund Deutsches Mädchen* [League of German Girls] left a life long memory with George. At the time he was fascinated with the differences between these organisations and the Boy Scouts, of which he was a member himself at the time.

Friedrichshafen; photographs of the HJ and BDM members encountered. One wonders what everyone was thinking when George took these photographs.

On a much better and somewhat lighter note the Collyer's Group also encountered two teachers from Ireland – both recently graduated from University and both in their first years of teaching. Their attitudes and dispositions reflected the students and staff from Collyer's. What they made of their German visit remains unrecorded.

The two teachers from Ireland, foreground; in the background is George, right, and Harry Chivers, left – a tour member.

Henry 'Harry' Thomas Chivers was the son of Henry and Rosetta Chivers of Wisborough Green, Sussex. He enlisted with the Royal Navy [service number [C/JX 356808] served on board *HMS Harvester*. He was an Ordinary Coder.

Jurua was ordered by Brazil in December 1937 from Vickers-Armstrongs, Barrow-in-Furness. The ship was laid down in June 1938 and she was purchased on September 5th, 1939 and renamed *HMS Handy*. The ship was launched on September 29th, 1939 and renamed *Harvester* in January 1940 as her original name was thought too liable to be confused with *Hardy*. *Harvester* was commissioned on May 23rd and briefly worked up at Portland Harbour before she was assigned to the 9th Destroyer Flotilla. The ship joined the Dunkirk evacuation on May 29th and returned 272 men to Dover

during the day. However, the situation at Dunkirk soon became too dangerous to risk the larger and more modern destroyers, so *Harvester* made no attempt to evacuate any troops during daylight hours on May 30th. This decision was rescinded and she sailed for Dunkirk on the night of May 30th/31st. En route she was narrowly missed by two torpedoes, but she rescued 1,341 men in two trips on May 31st and an additional 576 on June 1st. *Harvester* was lightly damaged by strafing German aircraft that same day and required repairs that were made at Chatham. On June 9th she was ordered to Le Havre, to evacuate troops, but none were to be found. She loaded 78 men at Saint-Valery-en-Caux on June 11th. Later in the month she escorted ships evacuating refugees and troops from Saint-Nazaire and St. Jean de Luz (Operation Ariel).

From July to September, *Harvester* was assigned to convoy escort duties with the Western Approaches Command and she rescued 90 survivors from the armed merchant cruiser *Dunvegan Castle* in late August. The ship, together with five other destroyers of the 9th Flotilla, was assigned to Plymouth Command for anti-invasion duties between September 8th and the 18th before returning to her role as an escort vessel. On October 20th, with help from her sister *Highlander*, she sank the German submarine *U-32*. *Harvester* rescued 19 survivors from the merchant vessel *Silverpine* in December 5th and 131 survivors from the *A.B.V. Crispin* in February 1941.

The ship was refitted at Barrow between March 18th and April 18th and then was assigned to Force H in Gibraltar where she escorted ships during Operations Tiger and Splice in May. *Harvester* was transferred to the Newfoundland Escort Force in June as her anti-aircraft capability was believed to be too weak. She was assigned to the 14th Escort Group upon her arrival at St. John's on July 1st. The ship was transferred back to the Western Approaches Command three months later and assigned to the 9th Escort Group. *Harvester* was converted to an escort destroyer during a lengthy refit at Dundee, Scotland, from January 30th to April 16th, 1942. She conducted sea trials of her Type 271 radar during May and then resumed her escort duties in the North Atlantic as flagship of Mid-Ocean Escort Force Escort Group B-3.

The ship was refitted at Liverpool between December 12th and February 11th, 1943. Whilst defending Convoy HX 228 on March 3rd, *Harvester* forced *U-444* to the surface and then rammed it. She was badly damaged by the ramming, but she rescued five survivors after the submarine sank. The next day, *Harvester* was torpedoed by *U-432* and broke in half. Nine officers and 136 ratings were lost, but the French corvette *Aconit* rammed and sank *U-432* herself and then rescued *Harvester*'s few survivors.

Harry was not among the survivors; he was killed that March 11th. His body was not recovered. He is commemorated on the Chatham Naval Memorial.

Some of the group on a mountain top in Switzerland with their guide.

The clothing attire contrasts with the snow covered ground even if in August!

George with one of the Irish teachers – George's photographic record of the tour is quite amazing.

It was back to Zurich for another two days before returning to Paris for yet another two day stop. It was during the return stay in Paris that George was severely reprimanded by one of the two Collyer's staff, Mr A. M. Wilson. George had left the accommodation and gone out to a shop nearby to buy chocolate but without permission from either of the two-accompanying staff. Mr Wilson was not impressed and advised George in no uncertain manner!

The Hotel where the group stayed [middle foreground] in their two visits to Paris; the Eiffel Tower is to the left of the buildings in the background.
Note how quiet the streets are – war was imminent and Parisians were aware; the tourist industry had gone the way Peace had gone.

The Group duly returned to England on August 21st – a mere ten days before the German invasion of Poland which, of course, initiated the war in Europe that would eventually become global. George's parents made little comment on his return other than welcoming him back and asking the many inquisitive questions parents ask their children on returning from a school trip. It was years later that George's sister spoke of their anxiety that George was touring France, Switzerland and Germany with war imminent!

George played a lot of sport at Collyer's – football, cricket, cross country running, fives and tennis. Playing in games meant a much longer day and frequently George would not get home until 7pm or so and then there was homework to do. The days were full! George excelled at games; he was captain of the under 14 team and also of the 2nd X1. He also played for the 1st XI – George's position being goalkeeper. He had the necessary agility and height. At cricket he played for the School's Under 14, 2nd XI and duly graduated onto the 1st XI. He also represented the school in cycling, tennis and fives. George was Under 14 and Under 15 school Champion in boxing for which his reward was a 2p [old pence] voucher [under 14] and 6p voucher [under 15] for the tuck shop! The 9p voucher for Champion at Under 16 level never materialised as George received the biggest hiding of his life in that final from one Ray Brookes.

George was just 14 years old and starting his fourth year at Collyer's when the War in Europe started. From that date his, and all other lives, completely changed. Food, sweets and clothing were all rationed and many items could only be obtained using coupons issued by the Government. The rationing in some cases was severe and many items would not be got until well after the War ended. Everywhere they went they had to carry gas masks in the expectation of the use of chemical warfare. Travel was severely restricted. German air raids and the 'Blitz' meant sleepless nights and George's schooling was mainly spent in Air Raid shelters. With just three hurricane lamps to provide light studying was at times difficult and tiring.

This was immediately accepted by everyone as everyone knew there was always someone worse off than themselves. The War also meant however excitement and everyone at Collyer's, as elsewhere in every school in the country, longed to join one of the Training Corps. In George's case this was the Army Defence Training Corps with a view to joining the Royal Air Force – George wanted to fly.

George donned a uniform for the first time when a member of the Air Defence Cadet Corps [late the Air Training Corps] at Collyer's in 1940. However, his wish to join Bomber Command as an air gunner never materialised as he failed the medical – George was, and still is, colour blind. He was offered ground staff duties but in a fit of pique George volunteered for the Army.

At Collyer's George wore the 'R.A.F. Wings' as a tie clip. This was not an approved addition to the attire of the student at the School. George frequently was told to remove his cherished 'wings'. The tie clip has survived and remains one of George's treasured possessions. A great memory of an ambition thwarted!

George sat the R.A.F. Apprentices' exam but although he did well insufficient applicants were taken. Later he would volunteer for flying duties [as an Air Gunner] but failed the medical examination due to colour blindness.

A school mate that did join the R.A.F. was John Raymond Grantham. He was the son of Herbert Thomas Grantham and Mabel Grace Grantham, of West Grinstead, Sussex. Sergeant Grantham, service number 1814726, was an Air Gunner. He served with the Royal Air Force Volunteer Reserve. He flew with 218th [Gold Coast] Squadron. He was killed on May 2nd, 1944 and is buried in Poix-de-Picardie Churchyard.

The crew of Short Stirling III EF259 HA-G RAF 218 Squadron, which came down on the Chably Operation on May 2nd, 1944. Photograph taken at Woolfox Lodge, England. April 1944. From left to right: Charles 'Jock' Weir, mid upper gunner; Ted Hawkins, flight engineer; Paddy Clayton, wireless operator; Flight Lieutenant Noel Stirling Eliot RAAF, pilot; Flying Officer Kevin John O'Neil (Jack) Lynch RAAF, bomb aimer; Johnny Grantham, rear gunner and Jack Hassett, navigator.

The aircraft this crew were flying was shot down on May 1st, 1944 while on a bombing raid over the Chambly railway marshalling yards, north of Paris. Those killed were Jack Hassett, Ted Hawkins, Paddy Clayton and Johnny Grantham. Flight Lieutenant Eliot was one of four survivors, including Charles 'Jock' Weir and Sergeant Wilson. The Germans buried the remains of the crew near the crash site but the bodies were reburied in the churchyard of the Church of St Denis at Poix after villagers had begun to put flowers at the crash site. Flight Lieutenant Eliot escaped from the aircraft by parachute and was picked up by members of the French Underground, surviving via the Comet (Comete) escape route, ending up in two camps of 152 Allied airmen, along with Jack Lynch and seven other Australian airmen, in the Forest of Freteval until liberation.

George has visited the grave of his good friend Johnny Grantham in the Churchyard of St Denis, Poix-de-Picardie.

Both Johnny and George wanted to be air-gunners, George failed the medical due to colour blindness.

Johnny Grantham's brother Tony was a well-known jockey

In 1950, the Queen Mother's horse Monaveen won the Grand National in Aintree, Liverpool. The jockey on the day was Anthony 'Tony' Graham His father was a Sussex horse dealer and livery man. Tony was born in 1921. He had ridden as an amateur before, competing successfully in both point-points and under Rules. So good was he that the Stewards of the day insisted that he turned professional, which he did. Monaveen was not Tony's first assault on the National - in 1948 he had ridden Lord Mildmay's Ultra Bene; they had parted company at the third.

Tony and Monaveen jumping the last at Hurst Park on the way to victory in the inaugural running of the Queen Elizabeth Handicap Chase on December 31, 1949.

Queen Elizabeth's interest in National Hunt racing had been triggered by champion amateur jockey Lord Anthony Bingham, who, in 1949, was staying as a guest at Windsor Castle for the Royal Ascot meeting. He suggested she bought a steeplechaser. Monaveen was the result. The horse was sent to Peter Cazalet's stable to be trained. Attached to Cazalet's stable was Tony. He thus became the first Royal jump jockey. Monaveen and Tony, watched by the young Princess Elizabeth, made his debut at Fontwell Park on October, 10th, 1949. He won, beating his two opponents with ease. However, Monaveen came to a sad end. Tony was slightly concussed riding Monaveen, again for the Queen Mother, when coming down at the water jump at Hurst Park on December 2nd, 1950. Monaveen was fatally injured. Tony did not ride again until January 5th, 1951.

Tony won the Cheltenham Gold Cup and several other good races on Gay Donald. He also rode Broken Tackle (Plumpton), Ryan Price's first ever winner. Having ridden over 400 winners, Tony retired from the saddle in 1958 to run a 140-acre beef farm and livery stable in Steyning, Sussex. He also trained a few point-to-pointers.

Tony retired to Newmarket-on-Fergus, County Clare in 1985. He died there in 1910 aged 89 years. Tony's son, Tom - named after Tony's father - became a jockey, and, aged 18, rode his first ever winner, Peyton Pearl, at Plumpton on October 26th, 1982. The Summer of 1940 remains of Historical importance for Britain – it was the Summer of the Battle of Britain. The skies over the Home Counties was filled with fighters and bombers as the Germans sought supremacy in the air as a precursor for an invasion and the Royal Air Force fought for supremacy to ensure there would be no Operation Sealion. The bulk of the Battle was fought over the countryside of the Home Counties with Sussex certainly no exception.

The Battle officially is recognised as being from July 10th until October 31st, 1940, which overlaps the period of large-scale night attacks known as The Blitz, that lasted from September 7th, 1940 to May 11th, 1941. George would have seen much of the Battle as it raged over him - whether it was German bombers or fighter 'planes for both sides engaged in dog fights.

One particular incident on July 19th brought the Battle that much closer to George – making it very personal. On his way home from school that Friday George saw a spit-fire come in low over West Grinstead Park – the fighter was in fact making a forced landing, being damaged. The hurricane came to a halt and George ran over to the fighter where it come to a stop. He helped the pilot out who muttered *bloody Germans*. George asked the pilot whether he would like a cup of tea which was answered in the affirmative. So, George started to walk the pilot back to the Lodge where his mother Mary would no doubt welcome the pilot and provide the necessary refreshments. For a 14-year-old it seemed as if all his dreams were coming true!

The excitement was short lived as a truck quickly arrived on the scene and the pilot was immediately taken away – so much for the refreshments and stories of derring-do! George does remember though the soldiers left on guard of the spitfire which had burned out for 2 to 3 days afterwards. What remained of the fighter was duly removed.

The events of July 19th, 1940 are corroborated by the work of the Cowfold Historical Society; the Society through its Chairman, Mike Burt provided the following further information on the incident -
Extract of an interview with John Jones, who was a schoolboy at Jolesfield school, Partridge Green during the war.
I remember we were running around where the spiked fences were out the front and a plane came along. It was a German bomber and it was obviously in trouble and there were three planes, whether they were Spitfires or Hurricanes I don't know, but they were taking turns at having a go at this bomber as it came by right over West Grin-stead. Then a Hurricane or Spitfire got just that little bit too bold and the German got him, he peeled off and came down in West Grinstead Park and I suppose the other two then sorted him out but by then it had gone out of sight. Us kids got on our bikes and went to West Grinstead Park, and as you go past the Old Tabby Cat there is a lodge house just there on the left, well it came down in that field. We were one of the first to get there. The pilot had crash landed and it was not many minutes before the army got there.

Extract from the diary of PC Albert Elliott who was the constable at Cowfold –
On 19 July 1940 went to West Grinstead Park where a Spitfire had been forced down on fire.
Pilot unhurt.

October 1941 – school group with French soldiers; George is in the middle of the photograph.

On leaving Collyer's in the Summer of 1941 George took up a position as a Superintendents' Assistant at Horsham Police Station. The job was mundane and not to George's liking or character. He longed to enlist.

The young George on leaving school - 17 years old.

Chapter 3 - At War

On March 19th. 1943 George travelled to Queen Street, Brighton, right, and enlisted. The interview with Lieutenant-Colonel Edmund Ferrers, D.S.O., resulted in a recommendation to serve with the Royal Engineers and train as a surveyor. George may have been disappointed that his ambition to serve with the Royal Air Force had been grounded; his father William would be equally as  disappointed that his son had joined the Engineers and not a Guards Regiment, specifically the Coldstream Guards to follow in his father's steps!

George remembers vividly the Lieutenant-Colonel reaching into his pocket as the interview was coming to a conclusion and very much as an afterthought, handed George a shilling – dated 1922. George was so proud of that shilling that it remains with him to the present day!

After all George had enlisted and was deserving of the 'King's Shilling'!

The King's shilling, sometimes called the Queen's shilling when the Sovereign is female, is a historical slang term referring to the earnest payment of one shilling given to recruits to the Armed forces of the United Kingdom in the 18th and 19th centuries, although the practice dates back to the end of the English Civil War. To "take the King's shilling" was to agree to serve as a sailor or soldier in the Royal Navy or the British Army. It is closely related to the act of impressment. The practice officially stopped in 1879, although the term is still used informally.

A recruit was still entitled to return the shilling until becoming subject to martial law upon formal attestation before a Justice of the Peace. At this point, a more substantial bounty was paid to the new recruit, which fluctuated from two guineas to a high of £23/17/6d in 1812. However, this payment generally was quickly lost to various duties and dues, such as uniform. The monetary amount of this bounty, which might be equivalent to half a year's wages for the average unskilled worker, was enough to persuade most potential recruits to join. Those who hesitated were often won over by making them intoxicated with strong drink. The bounty was lucrative enough for some to repeatedly desert, then reenlist: one man was hanged in 1787 for doing so 47 times.

The pay for a private in the English Army was originally one shilling a day. A soldier was expected to pay for food and clothing out of their wages after using the initial sign-up bounty to purchase their initial equipment. It was not until 1847 that a limit was placed on deductions, ensuring that each soldier was paid at least one penny (a twelfth of a shilling) a day, after deductions.

The terminology is first recorded in a note dated March 27th, 1707 by the antiquarian and diarist Thomas Hearne – *it is true, being unhappily engaged in mad company, he did take a shilling, but not with any intent of listing. Hopes to get out of the difficulty.* [*Remarks and Collections of Thomas Hearne*].

The earliest known instance of the King's Shilling is from *The Dublin Evening Post* of June 5th, 1828; quoting a *Galway paper* – *It appears that a military party had been beating up for recruits, during the day, in our streets. One of the Serjeants, or a Corporal (we known not which) was seen about 6 o'clock in the evening, at the corner of Cross-street, having a young fellow from the country, whom he claimed as his recruit. The poor fellow was unwilling to join his Majesty's service, but the Serjeant or Corporal, assisted by two other Serjeants and a Drummer, were hurrying him on to the Mayor and Magistrates office, with their swords and bayonets drawn, when a mob of country people took part with the alleged recruit, when a "slating" of no ordinary character ensued. Sticks and stones and green feathers flew aloft, and the heroes of Waterloo and Badajos were obliged to resign their laurels to poor Patrick. The young man protested most strongly, that the King's shilling was forced upon him – of so, we cannot sufficiently condemn the proceedings.*

Lieutenant Colonel Edmund Bromfield Ferrers D.S.O. ('Uncle'), the recruiting Officer, was born in 1878 and spent his entire military career as a Cameronian and was one of its best known officers, affectionately known as 'Uncle' to all who served in the regiment. Ferrers enlisted as a 2nd Lieutenant in 1899, serving with the 2nd Battalion during the South African War.

By the start of the First World War in 1914 he was in command of his beloved "B" Company. He distinguished himself at the Battle of Neuve Chapelle -
It was getting near the time for the guns to lift, and the subaltern was keeping an eye on his watch, when Gray-Buchannan nudged him and shouted, "There goes Ferrers." Looking up he saw Ferrers, monocle carefully adjusted and waving his sword, scrambling over the parapet 20 or 30 yards to the right; so calling to his men to follow, over he went to.

The Battle of Neuve Chapelle March 10th/13th, 1915, took, place in the First World War in the Artois region of France. The attack was intended to cause a rupture in the German lines, which would then be exploited with a rush to the Aubers Ridge and possibly Lille. A French assault at Vimy Ridge on the Artois plateau was also planned to threaten the road, rail and canal junctions at La Bassée from the south, as the British

attacked from the north. The British attackers broke through German defences in a salient at the village Neuve-Chapelle but the success could not be exploited.

During the Battle of Neuve Chapelle, he was wounded almost as soon as he crossed over the British line but re-fused to give up and contin-ued on to the German trenches where another hit forced him to stop. Still refus-ing to be carried back to safety by his men, instead he propped himself up against the German parapet for a bet-ter view and calmly lit a cigar. From his vantage point Fer-rers cheerfully encouraged his men by shouting; "Go on 'B' Company, I am dammed proud of you."

For his bravery and leader-ship at Neuve Chapelle, Fer-rers received the award of the Distinguished Service Order and he was also mentioned in Dispatches. He spent the next two years recovering from his injuries in England, all the time eager to get back to his beloved regiment. In February 1917 he rejoined the 2nd Battalion but struggled to cope on active service at the front whilst dealing with the effects of his injuries. After only two months he was forced to take a more peaceful role behind the front lines.

After the war he had recovered enough to accompany the 2nd Battalion to India, Iraq and Kurdistan, during which time he was able to resume command of "B" Company. After promotion to Lieutenant Colonel in 1923, Ferrers commanded the 1st Battalion and was in charge when they were posted to China in 1927. He held the command of the Ceylon Defence Force from 1931 until 1935. During the Second World War he was Recruiting Officer in Brighton from 1941 until illness forced his retirement in August 1942.

In his book 'Morale' John Baynes speaks very highly of Ferrers describing him as a - *Very remarkable character, he was always eccentric and had a most ready wit. At the same time he was the kindest of men, and had the very highest code of personal honour and integrity. His tactical and general military was not great, but when he came to command a battalion in the 1920s his ability to gain the devotion of the officers and men alike made him extremely successful.*

Lieutenant Colonel Ferrers died in February 1944 at the age of 66. He was unmarried, having spent his whole life entirely devoted to the regiment.

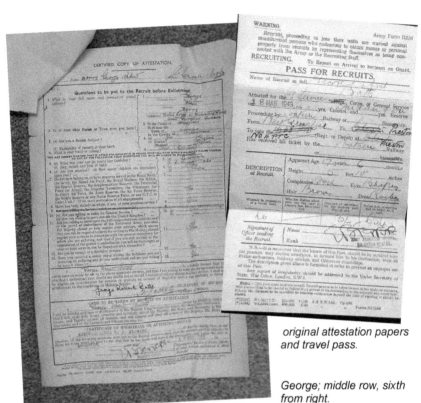

original attestation papers and travel pass.

George; middle row, sixth from right.

An effort by his Father and Uncles to have George serve with a Guards' Regiment ensured a sticker on his records noting that *under no circumstances must this sapper be transferred to any other Regiment without prior consultation with Officer i/c RE.*

Normandy, 1944

In late March George found hiself saying goodbye to the family and alighting the train to go to Fulwood Barracks at Preston, Lancashire - the home of the 'Loyals' to join No 4 Primary Training Corps for his initial six weeks training. George was just seventeen and a half years old – nothing more than a schoolboy. He had only left school just nine months before this and had never been away from home.

Square bashing, physical training, route marching, rifle drill, learning to use different weapons - Lee Enfield .303 rifle, Bren Gun, Sten Gun, grenades etc - followed. After six weeks George was adjudged to be a fully-fledged soldier, ready to serve King and Country in any theatre of war. He was posted to the Corps of Royal Engineers to be trained as Sapper. He did get into the Royal Engineers as he wanted but instead of going to be trained as a surveyor his posting was to train as a Stevedore D111!
From Preston the next place was Cardiff for Royal Engineer's Fieldwork training – learning to make knots, lashings splicings, make & erect derricks etc and become good Corpsmen.

This lasted for three weeks and then it was on to Tonwynlais (a Welsh Mountain near

Cardiff) to learn to live under canvas - this was nothing like camping with the Boy Scouts!. It poured with rain day and night for the completed ten days. They were always wet through and plodding around in six inches of mud. Guard duties were every other night for what reason he will never know – George cannot imagine anybody, friend of foe, wishing to go to that place.

At last back to Roath Park in Cardiff where they were informed that they were now fully fledged Royal Engineers, given their Cap Badge and shoulder flashes and would be getting their first unit posting. George was assigned to 1033 Dock Operating Company stationed in Liverpool.

However the Army can be kind! They were granted 7 whole days privilege leave. George travelled to his home in Sussex with full kit - Kit Bag, big pack, small pack, ammunition holders, water bottle, tin helmet, greatcoat, rifle (no 2 22042A) etc covered in mud from the mountain and looking like goodness knows what. Crossing London for the first time from Paddington to Victoria station in such a dishevelled state was quite an experience.

George eventually arrived home to a very proud Mum and Dad for seven whole days to be utterly spoiled and cosseted. He must have looked a sight when he arrived with an ill-fitting uniform muddy and unwashed. His father, the ex-Grenadier Guardsman took one look and said, *What in the hell Regiment are you in?!* He was disgusted with

George because of the appearance and promptly cleaned uniform and rifle, blancoed the equipment and polished the brasses.

George was never that smart again!!

For George's mother it must have been different feelings; George had left home an innocent 17 years old and here he was three months later almost a grown man fully equipped for action in war and not yet 18 years old. George never found out what her thoughts were at that time.

George saw a lot of his girlfriend, Eileen. They had been sweethearts at School when he was 15 and she was 14. Her father had just been killed in the Merchant Navy and was buried in Durban, South Africa. George will always remember her being at the railway station to say goodbye at 7.30am when he returned from leave. Like so many thousands of others they never knew if they would meet again – such were those times.

The leave time had flown by and George was on the train to join 1033 Dock Operating Company in Liverpool. Once again, he had to cross London in the rush hour with all his kit. George remembers how surprisingly rude and antagonistic the civilians on the Underground were

On arriving George found that the Unit were on exercise in North Wales so the next day he was carted off to Hope Mountain to join them. This really should be called Give up Hope Mountain as they lived under bivouacs - two ground sheets put together and shared between two - with the rain pouring down for the complete period. The training lasted for two weeks. All George remembers is being wet, cold, hungry and totally miserable. He remembers nothing of the type of training they were doing.

Then came his first taste of a route march – from Hope Mountain [left] to Chester – it seemed never ending and as if to spite them the sun shone for the first time in days and it was so hot. Here they boarded a train for Liverpool remaining there for a couple of weeks. The people of Liverpool were wonderful to them and made them so welcome. The next stop was Inverary in Scotland for Combined Operation Training on Loch Fyne [right] and in the Mountains. This was a three-week course and it rained nearly all the time. They were landing from small assault craft and unloading ships to shore by flat bottom canvas boats. In addition they were climbing the mountains around the area, route marches etc. They were fed up

with this as they always got wet through with the incessant rain and being in water up to their waists.

It was wonderful to leave here when the course finished but they went to Helensburgh, right, (again in Scotland) to live in Nissan Huts and very primitive condition. With rain again it was horrible. A few days after arriving here volunteers were requested to go on a course at the Transportation Training Centre in Longmoor in Hampshire. George had no idea what the course was but he put all the  advice of not volunteering for anything on one side and put his name down. All he envisaged was Longmoor was near home and I might get a few weekend leaves.

The course turned out to be for Advanced Special Section Training to be capable of going on enemy held territory raids etc. George was one of sixteen accepted from his Unit to attend the course and undertake this training for three months. It was quite a course! The first four weeks were solid Physical Training from 8am to 5pm each day, as we were told, to get us 150% fit. It did!! They did exercises, gym work, jumped and ran, climbed high walls with ropes, swung from tree to tree, did unarmed combat, covered a four-and-a-half-mile assault course 2-3 times per day. In the last week they covered a 32-mile cross-country run in PT kit and Army boots. Although it was tough George thoroughly enjoyed it.

They were now pronounced fully fit so proceeded to the next part of the course. This was learning about mines (German, Italian, British), explosives, booby traps, map reading and shooting with all types of weapons. Self-defence, unarmed combat, setting explosives to destroy building and bridges was interspersed with covering the Assault Course and rope climbing once per day. At the end of the four weeks they took an exam - a tough one - to see if they were competent.
George passed.

The final four weeks was really putting everything they had learnt into practice and preparing for actual future action against a real enemy. This entailed forced marches - 10 miles in two hours in full kit, a three-day endurance test - they covered 93 miles, sleeping in the rough, living off the land, suffering dummy attacks at all hours of the day and night. They also spent time clearing live mines - at night and in the day with detectors and prodding - dismantling live booby traps, using explosives, grenades, compass marching - day and night, being dumped in the middle of the night, goodness knows where and having to find your own way back to camp with no compass or map – and of course still going over the assault course every day. This training was every day 8am to 5pm plus three-night schemes per week. They had been searched to ensure that they had no money to buy anything - typical service instruction – on three shillings a day less various stoppages nobody ever had any money after pay day! This was quite an experience but was making them a force to be reckoned with.

A welcome five-day break came when we went to Battersea on a street-fighting course in the bombed buildings – climbing over roofs, along planks between buildings - top floor, swinging from one window to another four floors up, being bombarded with thunder flashes. Finally their baptism of being fired at with live ammunition – crawling along the ground while marksmen fired live bullets from Bren Guns 18 inches above heads. They were told to keep their heads down – and they did!

It was back to Longmoor for final few days training and then the Colonel's passing out parade on the Saturday morning and then they were given a weekend pass. They had an end of course party on the Friday night. How any of them were on the Parade the next morning George will never know!!

There were 32 starting the course, sixteen from George's unit and sixteen from a Port Maintenance Company. Twenty-one finished the course. The rest had broken bones and strains. After all these years – three quarters of a Century on - George still suffer from a pulled muscle he acquired on the assault course. Whilst on this course one of the instructors persuaded them to enter the Aldershot Command 10 mile-walking race. There were about 3,000 taking part. British, Americans, Canadian, Poles, French and other nationalities George's little Section won, and they were presented with medals. They went for a liquid celebration and while doing this somebody stole our medals. Such is life!

After the weekend it was a return to his Unit, 1033 Port Operating Company, R.E. at Wimborne in Dorset. After the hectic action of the course, life back with the Company seemed quite and mundane. They did one or two runs to keep fit but nothing exceptional – although the rest of the unit were not very happy with them as they always had to lead the runs and they were so much fitter than the rest.

George was then notified that he was not old enough to go overseas, as he was not 18 years old. This was heart-breaking, as it seemed that all the hard training - of which he was so proud - had been for nothing.

Thus, on Boxing Day, December 26th, 1943 George was one of a half dozen that boarded a train for they knew not where – only the NCO in charge had been told! Thirty-eight hours later they arrived at their destination – Glen Mavis near Airdrie in Scotland. This was to form a new Unit, 1049 Company. Their arrival time was 11pm and thus it was dark, cold and wet and, best of all, nobody knew they were coming and only a handful were there already. There were no food or drink other than hardtack biscuits and cocoa with no milk or sugar and they had no money or hope of a pay day. George really discovered what it was like to be really hungry!!

The people of Glen Mavis and Airdrie were wonderful to them. They must have been aware of their circumstances as they received many invitations to join them in their homes where they were well fed and watered. George will never forget one Annie Kennedy of Englefield Road who was like a mother to his mate Taff David and himself all the time they were there. A really wonderful lady – George still remembers her mouth-watering Scottish Potato cakes and home cooking.

The next few weeks were very busy forming the Company with all the red tape that is involved. They must have upset somebody high up as they were whipped off to Stranraer to help with building a new dock. This place they all felt was off the planet and they had no facilities whatsoever. They lived in Nissan Huts, washed in the mountain stream - that water is cold George remembers - and only sheep for company - leave the door open and you found them sleeping on the floor. The conditions were primitive. The ways of the army are indeed difficult to understand although George supposes there was some thought and ideas behind them. For what appeared no reason - although welcome - they were whisked off to Helensburgh (Scotland again!) and just cooled their heels for a while.

They were waiting for the camp at Inverary to become available so once again they went off to the camp on the edge of Loch Fyne for more Combined Operations Training. The weather was better and after the course George was much fitter and so the training did not seem so intense. However, it was tough. They went down the hills and mountains surrounding the Loch trained for various landing techniques from Assault craft (LCAs), flat bottom canvas boats and wading Arms drill, firing and use of explosives came into the training again. George enjoyed all of this. He does recall winning a lot of money playing cards and then losing it all again!

After this it was on to Blairhill School in Coatbridge, to complete the formation of the Company, and train incessantly to bond the Company together, and enable them to do all the tasks without thinking. Although they were working hard they had a wonderful time. The Scottish people were so good to them and once again George spent many happy hours at Annie Kennedy's house. George also recalls another local, Mary Gilchrist. She was a wonderful dancer and her friend's parents had a café – Taff and George never went hungry all the time they were there!!
After the war Mary wrote to the War Office to find out what had happened to me and to George's embarrassment and shame he never replied.

During this time all sorts of rumours were flying as to where they would be going – they knew it would be abroad. The Middle East or the Far East were the favourites. France never came into the guessing.

All good things come to an end and after the wonderful time in Scotland the whole Company were put on a train for they knew not where. This was another seemingly endless journey interspersed with rumours of where they were going. They knew it was somewhere down south. For George the best he heard it was to be a place in Sussex and they would be billeted in Knepp Castle. This was only two miles from his home so his imagination ran riot as to the easy time he would have in getting home frequently. By coincidence George's sister Marian was working there in the Women's Army. However this was not to be although their Headquarters did go there. They found ourselves in tents in the woods outside Hailsham in Sussex.

Everywhere they looked or went was swamped with troops – around them British and Canadian. Although they were totally unaware of the purpose of it all, it became patently obvious that they were preparing and mobilising for the Normandy Invasion. The security, secrecy, restriction on travel was intense and restricting. Parades and roll calls were carried out about three times per day to make sure nobody escaped! This route from their camp to headquarters passed his home and despatches had to be taken and collected from there very frequently. George managed to wangle the job as Dispatch Rider and thus used to call in home and spent many Saturday nights at home – absolute bliss! Many of George's unit had to travel to HQ with items and they always called in to George's home. George's mother was wonderful - she always found some food and tea for them in spite of rationing. George's Commanding and

Section Officer visited – as they said to ensure that the house was within the bounds they were allowed to travel!

George remembers Harry Harris, one of the drivers from London's East End calling in and then saying to him -
"Ain't you posh – you use table cloths"
He was later Court Martialled and sentenced for 10 years in prison for selling WD Equipment – mostly tyres.
Although they were told nothing and thus did not really know what was happening they guessed that it was going to be something big, as security got much tighter, special supplies were coming in, their transport being converted to drive through water and amphibious jeeps arrived.

As Despatch Rider George managed to get to his home on the weekend of May 20th and told his Mother that rumours said they were moving somewhere. His Mother dragged George into Horsham on the Saturday afternoon together with his sister to have photographs taken. Obviously the thinking was that George was off into action somewhere and could be killed!

Back in the camp on Sunday and packing all stores and records. There were check parades every two hours and, in a way general bedlam. But however everything seemed to be haphazard and lacking control, all things came together in a very orderly way.

Whilst at Hailsham it was, in a way, a very boring time as it was all mundane jobs and they did not know what was happening and, if they asked, they did not get an answer. When they had money, it was to the pub in Hailsham stagger home and wake up with a bad headache vowing the usual 'never again'. Around May 30th they were told they would be moving off somewhere, so it was down to the pub for a farewell do. George does not remember much of the evening, but he understands that he had the Section Officer - later their Commanding Officer - saluting him in the middle of the road about a dozen times. The next morning, he just said he would take George in hand wherever they landed up!

Security got tighter and at the absolute zenith from May 28th. There was a rumour that a visit from General Montgomery was likely for what they were told was to be words of encouragement. After standing in a field for two and a half hours awaiting his arrival and feeling thoroughly fed up the only thing George remembers about his pep talk was to the effect that they were about to make history, the way would be hard and although some would not make it they died serving King and Country.

On June 1st, every item of records, stores, kit, ammunition and explosives was packed. On June 3rd or 4th they were herded onto lorries and taken to Newhaven Docks to board a Landing Ship Infantry. George remembers seeing Assault Craft hanging from the sides but everything else is a blur. Troop movements were everywhere and the roads solid with lorries and other vehicles. All along the route people were lining the roads, waving, shaking hands and yelling good luck. Although there was strict secrecy, the local population guessed something was happening by the massive troop movements all going to various docks. At the time George does not think they took a lot of notice as their thoughts were elsewhere – but looking back at what the consequences could have been......................

D-Day

Once on board they had been told, and therefore knew, their destination that the big day had come, and they were to be a part of it. They settled down to the usual corny jokes and silly humour, which comes out of nervousness. Nobody admitted to being scared but....................George remembers thinking,
Why did I volunteer and then for the Special Section Course – I could be dead in a couple of days.

They were below deck on the ship so always in darkness. Thus, George has no idea what time they left Newhaven, but he thinks it was dark. Time did not mean a thing but with the ships movement they knew they were at sea.

They tried to sleep. Whether they did or not George has no idea but what seemed like no time, but must have been some hours, they were ordered up on the deck. A smoke screen was laid and someone shouted *Gas!*. There was panic to get their gas masks on and many got thrown all over the place. It was announced this was a false alarm, so they packed them up again – what a relief!

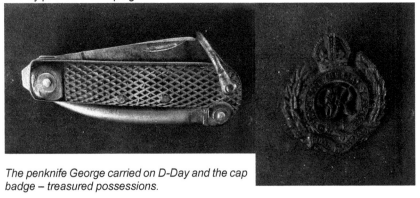

The penknife George carried on D-Day and the cap badge – treasured possessions.

The next order was to line up in readiness to board the Assault Craft. So there they were with small pack containing explosives, tin hat, loaded rifle, ammunition packs full and bandolier with more ammunition and more in a line across the deck. Once again nobody would admit it but they were all nervous and scared. But they all put on a brave face making a few of the usual corny wisecracks and (so-called) funnies. Really, George supposes it was being apprehensive as they were all unaware of what they were going into but knowing that they could – and would - be dead within an hour or so.

George's everlasting memory is of standing waiting to board the Assault Craft with a whole tin of Corned Beef in one hand and a hunk of bread covered with thick butter in the other (George still has a liking for corned beef) thinking
if I am killed this is the condemned man's last meal – I wish it was some of my Mum's cooking.
As it turned out this was the last bread he had for about four months – they lived on hard tack biscuits.

The order came to get into the Assault Craft. It was rising up and down with the swell and they had to climb down rope netting to board. The rising was a phenomenal number of feet, so they had to judge the right time to jump and hope for the best. A few misjudged it and finished being crushed between the landing craft and the ship. George remember their Sergeant Major shouting -
For F...s sake jump.

George reckons that they were about 4 - 5 miles from the shore. When they were all in the craft it was off for the shore. George cannot describe his feeling other than saying it was frightening, apprehensive and, in a way, a feeling of doom but hopeful and determined to survive. He feels sure that they all prayed for the Divine help in what they had to face. Obviously, everyone in that craft knew they could be dead any minute. George thought of home of his Mother and Father, his sister Marian and girl friend Eileen and that he may never see them again.

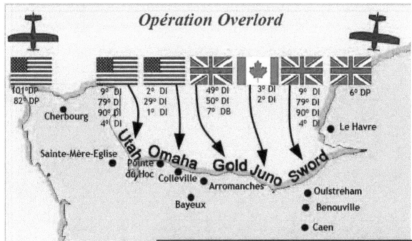

He was landing on Gold Beach.

In what seemed no time at all the ramp went down and the phenomenal training that they had undergone took over. Although scared George was quite cool and determined to survive. His special training did help as everything was done automatically. They jumped into about four feet of water and ran up the beach looking for any cover that was available. The Germans were using the houses at Le Hamel

to fire along the beaches with machine guns, which caused a lot of casualties. One gun in particular took a long time to silence. They had been well briefed on what they had to do, and I think they abided by these instructions. In the water there had been obstructions with mines attached and the beach and land at the end of the beach was mined.

From the early hours of the morning and now the noise was incredible, large naval guns had been firing offshore, German gun emplacements returning fire. The R.A.F. had and was carrying out sorties. The most memorable sight was seeing gliders and aircraf going across the skies.

Dead bodies, mutilated bodies and bits of bodies, were in the sea and everywhere on the beach. This has been well chronicled so George will not go into detail. Fortunately the human mind blanks out many of the incidents and sights and although they stick in the mind happily the main ones are the amusing incidents. D-Day was initially a dreary, misty day made so because of the smoke and dust from falling shells and the smoke. Because of his training and briefing George knew exactly what to do and was lucky enough for this to happen.
He was one of the lucky ones who survived the initial landing but so many did not.

Thus George had arrived in France.

Normandy

The initial few days in Normandy were hectic and George's unit was unloading stores from DUKWs, which were running a continual route from ship to shore. Being in 'lines of communication' branch of the Royal Engineers they remained at Arromanches while the front line moved on and as this got further away their life became easier with less likelihood of being killed. The main worry was a few German snipers hanging around and German aircraft coming over.

We had seen 'big lumps of concrete' and other weird looking objects being towed across the Channel and had no idea what they were. All sorts of rumours spread as to their use, but little did they know that they were to form Mulberry Harbour and that they would be working on this for a few months. This harbour was an incredible invention and enabled them to unload supplies, ammunition, land reinforcements, despatch wounded and Prisoners of War, in short anything that goes with a normal port. The sight of the wounded going through and the extent of many of their wounds were terrible. This memory has stayed with George all of his life and he hopes and pray that most of them recovered. It must be realised that they were all very young men and many of these lives had been ruined forever.

George remembers two squaddies stealing a DUKW and endeavouring to get away to return to the UK in it. They did not get very far!

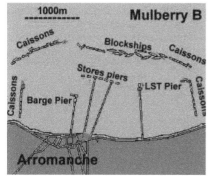

The unit were living in an orchard near Arromanches in bivouacs and going to Mulberry Harbour to carry out 12-hour shifts. Life was routine and reasonably uneventful.

The big storm of June 19th/20th, which destroyed the American Mulberry Harbour and damaged the one at Arromanches, was frightening and could have jeopardised the whole campaign but the British one was fully repaired very quickly.

The Harbour was surrounded with Barrage Balloons and at night a Box Barrage of Anti-Aircraft fire was used to deal with German aircraft who obviously wished to bomb the Harbour.

Due to these efforts no bomb was ever dropped on it, but a heck of a lot of shrapnel used to come down and ping on the metal deck.

George's unit worked on the Mulberry Harbour throughout the Battle of Normandy and continued until October when it had outlived its usefulness and ports in Belgium had been taken.

Thus, the sojourn at Arromanches came to an end and they moved across North France.

The time there had been tough, they had worked hard and always kept supplies and ammunition going forward. George believes that they were fortunate in being static and doing a particular job, but as in all walks of life various amusing events occur.

When based at Arromanches George's company were billeted in tents to the immediate south of the town. They were in a field next to a large farm dominated by a chateau, below, which was used as a medical centre and hospital.

Across from where they were billeted was a field with a water pump in the middle of it. Every morning two young French ladies used to come there to wash – this was the only cabaret and entertainment they had!

The outbuildings of the farm and the field to the right where the pump was sited.

On another occasion, George's great friend Len, later his best man, and George decided they would like a change of diet, so they went off on a hunt for chicken. They came across a farm house and as George knew a little school boy French it was decided that he would occupy the farmer at the front while Len nipped round the back and grabbed a couple of chickens.

The approach from the west to Tracy-sur-Mer, the scene of the 'chicken' incident.

All was going well until one chicken escaped from Len and made one heck of a noise. Unfortunately, the farmer had a double-barrelled shotgun!! It must have been quite a sight to see two brave British soldiers legging it down the road chased by an old farmer. Fortunately, George believes he had no ammunition!
A few days later, they did manage to get a couple of chickens!

The farm above and to the right in the image below.

North West Europe 1944/1945

The Normandy Campaign ended with the breakout in August, 1944. The Allies moved quickly across France and towards Belgium and Germany. George remembers the weeks as quite exhilarating. They moved across the country in all sorts of transport stopping for nights at various places en-route. One night they stayed at Poix-de-Picardie where George visited the grave of his friend [Sergeant] Johnny Grantham. He had been killed on a bombing mission on May 2nd, 1944. Another night was spent at Poperinghe in western Belgium. It was here that George and Len were grabbed by the local Resistance who believed them to be German spies. Their throats were about to be cut. It is peculiar how the French you were taught in school can quickly be recalled to get one out of an awkward position!

The 'Mulberry Harbour' created at Arromanches had by now outlived its usefulness. George's unit was moved on to the Belgian coast to work on the harbours of Ostend, Antwerp [right] and Bruges.

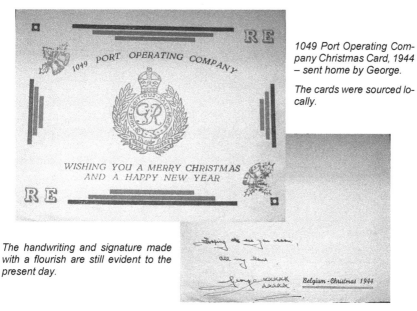

1049 Port Operating Company Christmas Card, 1944 – sent home by George.

The cards were sourced locally.

The handwriting and signature made with a flourish are still evident to the present day.

Belgium - Christmas 1944

On Leave

The war in Europe may have been coming to an end but the war with Japan continued and so George would soon find himself on the way to the Far East. But, having been in France and Belgium since June 6th, 1944 he was due leave home to England in March 1945.

George left Antwerp in early March 1945 for fourteen day's leave. To his delight this was extended by a further week and further extended by another two days as the ship destined to carry them from Liverpool to Mumbai [Bombay] was not ready for the voyage with the delay due to slow loading.

George took advantage of the leave and made his way to Horsham where he would meet up with his family and with Eileen – not seen for the best part of ten months.

The Far East

The War in Europe may rapidly have been coming to a conclusion but the hostilities continued unabated in the Far East and Japan still needed to be defeated. Therefore, George's unit was among those withdrawn from Europe and prepared for action in the Far East Campaign.

They were mobilised once again and so George sailed for India on June 7th on the *Johnann van Oldenbarnevelt*. The vessel was built in the Netherlands and sailed regularly between Amsterdam and the East Indies. The ship served as an allied troopship during World War II. She was sold to the General Steam Navigation Company of Greece in 1962.

Renamed *Lakonia*, the ship completed a successful cruise from Southampton to the Canary Islands in April 1963, planned as the first of a long series. On December 19th, she departed Southampton for an 11-day Christmas cruise with 646 passengers and 376 crew under Captain Mathios Zarbis. She caught fire and sank north of Madeira on 22 December 22nd, 1963, with the loss of 128 lives.

From there it would be onwards to Malaya for the intended landings there. George remembers well the journey – the Bay of Biscay was rough, the Mediterranean peaceful, quiet and beautiful, the Suez Canal interesting, the Indian Ocean rough and life on board the ship restful but boring and tedious. The voyage took some 34 days in total even if travelling the quicker route through the Suez Canal. The journey George remembers was interesting in some instances but mostly incredibly boring. For much of the time it was a case of wondering what was at the end of the voyage.

Arriving in Mumbai was a new experience; the weather was hot and humid. The so-called tropical kit was a sight to behold. George's shirts were three sizes too large for him, the shorts were of pre-1914 design and vintage with legs that turned up for the day and down for the night. Everyone in the Unit had different looking items of differing shades of khaki and nothing fitted.

The Unit looked an absolute shamble rather than a fighting unit of the Army.

They were immediately transferred to a train to take them the 60 odd miles to their acclimatising camp at Haylan. George remembers it as a dreadful place. There was a further six weeks of training. Many suffered from dysentery. Then it was back to Mumbai.

Mumbai, August 2nd, 1945

On arrival they were readied and mobilised for invasion. The military plan – Operation Zipper - was to invade Malaya in two small places – Port Moresby and Port Swattenham. Casualties were expected to be high. They would be sailing through the Straights of Malacca with the Japanese manning the banks on either side with the distance apart being six miles or so. The actual invasion would be by landing craft. They were convinced they would not survive and the Japanese would see off the invasion.

However, the Atomic Bombs were dropped and the Japanese surrendered.

P. & O. S.S. RANCHI, 16,600 TONS GROSS.
India Mail and Passenger Service.

The SS Ranchi – the ship that took the unit from Singapore to Java. The crew consisted of 4 Officers and 5 o/ranks!

Private order insignia worn by George when in the Far East.

S.E.A.C.

S.E.A.C.

George fraternising with a local.

As the War in the Far East was now over they were utilised to go to Prisoner Of War Camps and help and release the prisoners, both civilian and military. It is impossible to describe the sights they met, George recalls, seeing the suffering those poor inmates had suffered. He remembers carrying men who were barely four stone in weight but who were nonetheless so grateful for the help they received. It remains difficult to comprehend how such cruelty and suffering could have been done.

Our Unit was subsequently used to guard Japanese prisoners-of-war and eventually to operate the docks at Singapore.

The Camp – all under tent and most tranquil after the travails of War.

George with Brian Makepiece, the Straits of Johore in the background…

….and with palm trees as background!

George, centre, in casual mode

80

Life became very pleasant, relaxing and bearable. But they remained a long way from home. They were then whisked off to Java to deal with the situation there and hand back the control and order created to the Dutch. Once that was done it was to Malaysia. The Communist guerrilla War was starting up during their last 8-10 months out there. It was dangerous to travel outside a built-up area and venture into the countryside. After they left the War did intensify, the beginning of a very nasty War.

Despite the tranquillity there were casualties from disease and the general conditions – the funeral of Peter Newman. George was part of the firing squad.

Six decades plus later George had the opportunity of visiting the grave when on a visit to the Far East.

The shortage of troopships ensured the sojourn in the Far East was longer than it should have been. There were thousands of servicemen to be returned to England and only so many ships to utilise. George was assigned to 'Demob 54' but was re-assigned to 'Demob 53', and so was going home earlier than expected. On July 4th, 1947 the troopship was finally available – the MV Dilwara. To George's surprise Len Higgins was on the same ship – Len had been sent to Japan for the previous three months when George was sent to Singapore; now they are back together again!

Dilwara was built by Barclay Curle & Company, Glasgow. She was launched in October 1935 and finished in 1936. She was owned by the British India Steam Navigation Company from 1936-1960. She was the first purpose built British troopship since 1867 and could accommodate 104 First Class passengers, 100 Second Class, 164 troops' families and 1,154 troops.

In 1939, when war broke out, she was in the Indian Ocean homeward bound. On September 16th, 1939 she collided with the Blue Funnel Line Stentor and undertook repairs at Gibraltar until late November. During 1940-1941 she was used as a troopship from South Africa to Egypt and took part in the evacuation of Greece. In 1942 she was present at the Madagascar landings. In 1943 she took part in the Sicilian campaign. In 1945 she was involved in the liberation of Burma but on June 8th 1945 was mined off Rangoon, reaching port with minor damages. She was the HQ ship during surrender operations at Singapore.

in 1949 she was refitted by her builders with a lower troop capacity and with bunks instead of hammocks and re-entered service in October 1950. Most of her employment was now between the UK and the Far East, including service in the Korean War and the Suez Campaign. Her trooping contract terminated in 1960; she remained in service until November 1971 when she was sold to be broken up by Tung Cheng Steel Co Ltd, Kaohsiung, Taiwan.

Back to 1947 and for George and from the decks of the ship there was the most marvellous view of the Far East to date – the disappearing view of Singapore as the ship pulled out into open sea.

Stopover at Suez....

Rest and recuperation...

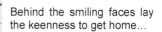

Behind the smiling faces lay the keenness to get home...

A couple of days' sojourn and onwards....

They eventually arrive in Southampton on July 2nd, disembarked and assumed it was straight home – but no!

The first thing was to go through Customs where some were searched. George had to pay seventeen shillings [two days' pay] duty on a couple of nylon stockings! The Customs Officer was quite apologetic, but he insisted on payment. Not having the money there which meant borrowing from a friend.

Thus, the welcome home!

From there it was onwards to Inkerman Barracks in Aldershot and 'demob'. The transport provided were 'three tonners'. The journey should have taken sixty minutes, but the Polish drivers managed half that time. There was feeling of surrealism – most had it through the war with minor wounds if at all and here was the distinct possibility of much worse.

They were given a suit, hat, shoes and raincoat, final pay [£62] and a travel warrant. They did have to return the kit they were in. Thus, George's service finished on July 4th, 1947 – but he remained on the reserve list.

George had been away for almost five years, had been to several countries, seen sights that were wonderful and others so horrific that one should never experience and certainly would last for the whole of his life. He had made many friends, lost many friends, experienced comradeship that cannot be explained and remains with him forever, determined in the hope that future generations will not lose their youth the way they did and that all the sacrifices made by so many were not in vain.

George had left home nothing more than a schoolboy but returned an experienced grown man very much, having lost many friends and comrades.

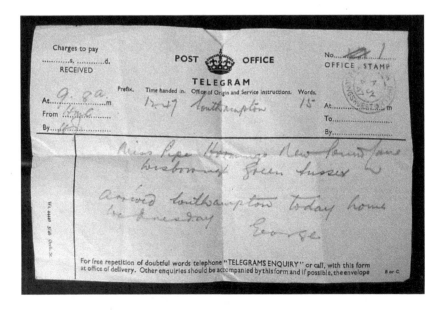

Chapter 4 - The Family Man

Kathleen Eileen Pipe – known as Eileen – was born on February 13th, 1927 in East Ham, the daughter of William Charles and Edith [Bridger] Pipe. William was born on July 10th, 1893. He was an omnibus driver. He served with the Royal Army Service Corps in the Great War as a driver. Edith was born on July 23rd, 1899. The couple married in 1922.

The wedding photograph of William and Edith, 1922.

Edith [Bridger] Pipe *Annie Bridger*

William was the eldest son of Charles and Hannah Pipe of Firgrove Stables, Farnham in Surrey. Charles was born in 1869 in Barnwell, Surrey. He was a domestic coachman. Hannah was born in 1866 in Reigate, Surrey. The couple married in 1892 and had six children – William, Alfred Frank, born in 1896, Edwin Walter, born in 1899, Albert, born in 1901, Dorothy, born in 1905 and Sidney, born in 1907.

From left to right - Annie, Edith and Eileen.

Edith was the youngest daughter of George and Annie Bridger. George was born in 1866 in Normandy, Surrey. He was a blacksmith. Annie was born in Kildare [Ireland] in 1867. The couple married in 1890 and had four children – Annie, born in 1891, William, born in 1893 who followed in his father's trade as a blacksmith, Lillie Eleanor, born in 1896 and Edith Pridmore, born in 1899. The family home was Willey Green, Normandy, Surrey. Normandy is near Guildford. Edith died on December 12th, 1989. Her probate was valued at £143,484.

Edith and William Pipe on the right with Annie centre back and Eileen in front of her.

Edith during the Great War; on War Service.

NATIONAL
REGISTRATION
ACT, 1915.

This Certificate must be signed and carefully preserved by the person to whom it is issued.

If the place of residence of the holder of the Certificate is changed otherwise than temporarily, the Certificate must be handed in at a Post Office or sent or delivered to the Clerk of the Council of the Borough, Urban or Rural District in which the new residence is situate (or, in Scotland, the Town or County Clerk), with the new address written in the space below. A fresh Certificate will be supplied in due course.

Space for new address:

This is to Certify that

(a) *Edith Bridger*

(b) *Dressmaker* (ll)

(c) of *Lynwode 23 Peperharow Rd*
GODALMING,

has been Registered under the
NATIONAL REGISTRATION
ACT, 1915.

Signature
of
Holder: } *Edith Bridger*

GOD SAVE THE KING.

(a) Name.   (b) Occupation.   (c) Postal Address.

William served with the Merchant Navy [service number 164625]. Because of his lengthy times at sea the family moved to Sussex to be nearer her mother's family in Godalming, Surrey. Eileen attended the Girls' High School in Horsham. William worked for the Union-Castle Line primarily as an attendant.

The Union-Castle Line was a British shipping line that operated a fleet of passenger liners and cargo ships between Europe and Africa from 1900 to 1977. It was formed from the merger of the Union Line and Castle Shipping Line. Union-Castle named most of their ships with the suffix "Castle" in their names; the names of several inherited from the Union Line were changed to this scheme (for example, *Galacian* became *Glenart Castle*) but others (such as *Galeka*) retained their original name. They were well known for the lavender-hulled liners with red funnels topped in black, running on a rigid timetable between South-ampton and Cape Town. Every Thursday at 4pm a Union-Castle Royal Mail Ship would leave Southampton bound for Cape Town. At the same time, a Union-Castle Royal Mail Ship would leave Cape Town bound for Southampton. In 1922 the line introduced its Round Africa service, a nine-week voyage calling at

twenty ports en route. Alternate sailings travelled out via the Suez Canal and out via West Africa.

The combined line was bought by Royal Mail Line in 1911, but continued to operate as Union-Castle. Many of the line's vessels were requisitioned for service as troop ships or hospital ships in the First World War, and eight were sunk by mines or Ger-man U-boats. The Royal Mail Line ran into financial difficulties in the 1930s, culminat-ing in the prosecution of its director Lord Kylsant, and Union-Castle Line became an independent company again with Vernon Thomson as Managing Director. Many vessels were again requisitioned in the Second World War. Three – *Dunnottar Castle, Carnarvon Castle, Dunvegan Castle* became armed merchant cruisers. *Pretoria Castle* (1939) was also first requisitioned as an armed merchant cruiser, but later served as an escort carrier.

After the war the line made good use of its three ships converted to troop transports to facilitate carrying the vast number of emigrants seeking new lives in East and South Africa. When they ran out of berths the line set up its own internal travel agency to book passages on other lines and even air services. The mail service to South Africa, curtailed during hostilities, recommenced with the sailing of *Roxburgh Castle* from Southampton in January 1947. The Union-Castle Line merged with Bullard King and Clan Line in 1956 to form British & Commonwealth Shipping, and then with South African Marine Corporation (commonly referred to as SAF-Marine) in 1973 to create International Liner Services, but maintained its separate identity throughout. Its shipping operations ceased in 1977.

A life working for a shipping Line meant months away from family and home. The sole method of communication were letters and postcards sent home or sent to the ship William was then working on.

INTERMEDIATE MOTOR VESSEL "LLANGIBBY CASTLE."

On the Llanigby Castle, off Dunkirk en-route to London having called at Southampton.

Many thanks for cards sent to Southampton ... hope Eileen and yourself are still well ...

William with the ship's cat.

89

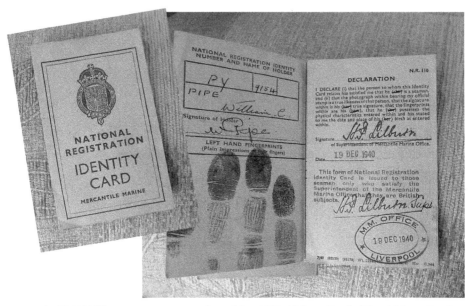

In 1941 William was a crew member of the *M.V. Athlone Castle*. The *Athlone Castle* was built in 1936 by Harland & Wolff at Belfast with a tonnage of 25564grt, a length of 696 feet, a beam of 82 feet 5 inches and a service speed of 20 knots. She was a sister ship of the *Stirling Castle*, and was launched by the Princess Alice, wife of the Earl of Athlone, a former Governor General of South Africa, on November 28th, 1935.

On April 14th, 1937 she arrived Cape Town with a new outward bound record of 13 days and 51 minutes. On November 5th, 1937 she was the first mail ship to call at

Buffalo Harbour at East London and on December 22nd, 1938 inaugurated the 14 days or under 'Accelerated' schedule as stipulated in the 1936 mail contract.

She was requisitioned for war transport in December 1940. In six years of War she would carry a total of 148,113 troops. In 1940 she was the commodore ship of a Union-Castle convoy made up of *Arundel Castle*, *Windsor Castle*, *Winchester Castle*, *Durban Castle* and *Capetown Castle* to carry South African troops to Suez following the outbreak of fighting in North Africa. During 1943, together with her sister, she trooped between the USA and UK carrying some 150,000 troops without any serious incident. She was under the command of Captain Andrew Alderson between September 1940 and February 1944.

In 1946 she underwent a refit in Belfast and continued in service until August 6th, 1965 when she concluded her 141st voyage at Southampton. Her sale had already been negotiated and ten days later she sailed for Kaohsuing in Taiwan where she arrived on September 13th for breaking up by the China Steel Corporation.

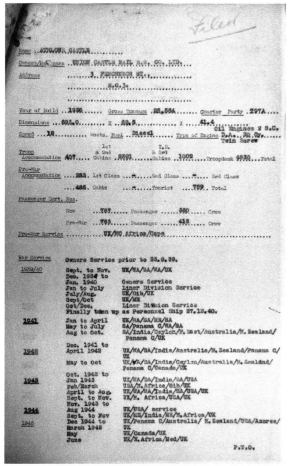

War Service record of the M.V. Athlone Castle

In the opening months of 1941 the *Athlone Castle* was part of a convoy that sailed from England to South Africa and onwards to Suez and back.

Convoy WS 5B sailed in three sections, from the Bristol Channel (4 ships), Liverpool (6 ships), and from the Clyde (11 ships). The Bristol Channel and Liverpool sections, after their juncture, were oblige to anchor in Moelfre Bay from January 8th through to the 11th, prior to their final rendezvous with the Clyde section; they had therefore to enter Belfast Lough to complete with fresh water. Sailing from the Lough, and the junction with the Clyde ships, took place on the 12th. The cruisers *Australia* and *Naiad* provided Anti Air-craft protection while the ships lay in Moelfre Bay, Anti Submarine protection was by the destroyers *Harvester* and *Highlander* and the sloop *Wellington*.

The convoy sailing plan was:

11 DUCHESS OF BEDFORD or ORBITA?	21 CAPE-TOWN CASTLE	31 EM-PRESS OF JA-PAN	41 ATHLONE CASTLE (Commo-dore)	51 BRITTANIC	61 ORMONDE (Vice Commo-dore) DURBAN CAS-TLE also shown here	71 DUCHESS OF RICH-MOND
12 FRANCONIA	22 NEA HEL-LAS	32 WINDSOR CASTLE	42 EMPRESS OF AUS-TRALIA	52 WINCHES-TER CAS-TLE	62 DUCHESS OF BEDFORD OR ORBITA?	72 HIGHLAND CHIEF-TAIN=
	23 ARUNDEL CASTLE	33 MON-ARCH OF BER-MUDA	43 PENNLAND		63 SAMARIA	73 HIGHLAND PRINCESS
						74 DUCHESS OF YORK

The convoy arrived at Capetown on February 8th and Durban on the 11th. The constituents of the convoy changed somewhat on sailing from South Africa, sailing from Capetown on the 12th and from Durban on the 15th. On the junction of the two sections, the formation became:

11 WINCHESTER CASTLE	21 EMPRESS OF JAPAN	31 ATHLONE CASTLE	41 FRANCO-NIA	51 ORMONDE	61 BRITANNIC	71 DUCHESS OF RICHMOND
12 DURBAN CAS-TLE	22 EMPRESS OF AUS-TRALIA	32 ARUNDEL CASTLE	42 NEA HEL-LAS	52 WINDSOR CASTLE	62 CAM-ERONIA	72 ORBITA
13 CAPETOWN CASTLE	23 DUCHESS OF BED-FORD	33 MON-ARCH OF BERMUDA		53 PENN-LAND	63 SAMARIA	73 NIEUW HOL-LAND

Arriving off Mombasa on the 21st, four of the Convoy sailed for that port.. The remainder of the convoy escorted by Australia, proceeded to Suez arriving on March 3rd.

The amended formation after detachment of the Mombasa ships being:

PRIVATE 11 WINCHESTER CASTLE	21 DUCHESS OF BEDFORD	31 ATHLONE CASTLE	41 FRANCO-NIA	51 BRITANNIC	61 DUCHESS OF RICH-MOND
12 DURBAN CAS-TLE	22 PENNLAND	32 ARUNDEL CASTLE	42 NEA HEL-LAS	52 CAMERONIA	62 ORBITA
13 CAPETOWN CASTLE		33 MONARCH OF BERMUDA		53 SAMARIA	63 NIEUW HOLLAND

The return journey to South Africa was equally uneventful.
Athlone Castle was back in South African waters entering Durban in early April 1941.

ATHLONE CASTLE.
Periods under repair since March 1941.

Port.	Arrd.	Sld.	Days Repairing.	Nature of Repairs.
'41.				
Durban	4/4	12/5		Drydocking & voyage repairs.
L'pool	7/6	28/6	16	Voy. repairs.
Greenock	25/10	9/12	33	Engine & voy.repairs.
1942.				

From April 4th until May 12th was in dry docks undergoing repairs at Durban as the records indicate.

It was here in Durban where William died – injuries laceration of spleen at Addington Hospital, Durban on May 9th, 1941. On shore leave, he stepped off the pavement to

93

let oncoming pedestrians the right of way – the man he left come was of Native descent. Unfortunately, William was struck by a taxi and was knocked down with fatal injuries as it turned out to be.

The first functional hospital in Durban, "The Bayside Hospital", was situated on the Victoria Embankment at the site now occupied by the Supreme Court. In 1879, the new Government Hospital was built at the present site, and named after Rt. Hon. Henry Addington who held the post of Prime Minister of Great Britain in 1801. The name Addington originates from that of the Estate of the late BWH Addison, the first Superintendent of the hospital in present site in 1878. The other opinion about the origin of the name, says that a friend of Mr Addison was instructed in 1860 to build a township in Durban to be called Addington Township.

Additions to the Hospital complex were ongoing, and the hospital as it stands today was completed and officially opened on November 10th 1967. As one gazes out at the sea from the high rise building, one can see close to shore the remains of the wreck of a 4,500 ton merchant ship, the Ovington Court, that ran aground on the beach in front of the Hospital on November 25th 1940. Doctors were sent to the beach to render first-aid. The wards were cleared and many of the survivors were admitted. It was unbelievable that anyone could have been drowned so near the shore. This was the first of many emergency situations that the Hospital has responded to.

The pins worn by Eileen during the war –
the R.E pin for George,
the M.N. pin in honour of her father William.

94

*William's funeral
in Durban….*

*He does not have a
CWGC Headstone.*

Working Life

Now dreams had come to fruition and it was home for good or so George thought. He would be later called back to do Z Training for two weeks. This was an utter waste of time and money and the least said about that the better George believes. Although whilst in the Army there had been some tough, frightening and terrible times there had been some enjoyable and rewarding experiences. The comradeship in the tough and good times and the friendships cemented had carried them through all those years, and, as it turned out, for many years afterwards.

Now, immediate post-War they were by themselves with no one to understand the feelings and, of course, doubts started springing up. George had only left school for a few months before volunteering for the Army at seventeen and a half and so had no experience of grown up life and the implications of it. Four of the previous five years he had been away from home and like so many others, three or four of these years had been spent in a combat zone. The War had been over for nearly three years by the time George was demobbed.

So many memories had started to fade.

Although his Mother, Father and sister were all living at home the family were nonetheless living out in the countryside and so George felt very isolated and deserted. His only job to date had been as a Police Superintendent Clerk at Horsham Police Station. Then he had the intention of joining the Police Force when the opportunity presented itself. This he was offered but rightly or wrongly George now declined – he had had his fill of uniforms! – and now, he was unemployed.

Whilst George was out in Malaya and Java various information had come to him about employment after demobilisation. Among these was to visit the Office of the Ministry of Labour where he had been informed that a special department was there to help returning ex-servicemen and would find job vacancies. George duly visited the Office in Bishopric in Horsham in September, 1947 where there were two staff. George explained the position he was in and stated he was looking for a job. The result – he was laughed at. So that was that; it seemed that Government Information was easier to transmit to the Far East than to offices and Civil Servants in places such as Horsham.

George was on his own.

George could not settle down in the countryside even if he was fussed over by everyone in the family. There was though too much time to dwell on the recent past and it was necessary to think really hard about the future. George therefore decided to move to London. He managed to get a job as a Temporary Grade III Civil Servant in the Accounts Department at Burlington House, London W1.

George was paid £4 2 shillings and 6 pence a week with one and a half hours compulsory overtime per week. After deduction this came to £4 3 shillings and 10 pence. He rented a room in Earls Court which set him back £1 10 shillings a week. This was a terrible place George recalls; it was basic with gas light, gas fire and cooking ring – the water tap and toilets were two floors below. George was often broke and he walked from Earls Court to Piccadilly Circus and back at least twice a week. Lunch, when it happened, was a cheese sandwich and the evening meal consisted of whatever he could scrounge from home at the weekend and all cooked on one saucepan. It was not the best but George was determined not to give in.

The work was preparation of the salary sheets for monthly paid Civil Servants. The sheets had to balance and so were checked by two other staff. This was obviously a job with no long-term prospects so after three months George left. His next employment was a clerk with the Singer Machine Company at the Head office in the City. The work was interesting, the staff friendly and the conditions and prospects good. In addition, George had a lot of contact with the public on the telephone dealing with enquiries and such like. The vast majority of callers were polite and affable, but George does remember the few who were rude and unappreciative. George did learn a lot in his time here.

George gradually moved up the ranks serving as a junior auditor, then senior and eventually being the Chief Clerk controlling a large staff. There was always changes and new developments. George moved to be Sales Office Manager with an office in Oxford Street, opposite Selfridge's. George was subsequently moved to a new sales department to increase sales into other outlets other than just the Company's own shops.

After seventeen years with Singer's George left the Company and took up a position as Sales Manager to the Italian Compony, Borletti Veglia who were based in Milan. George found this very much to his liking as there were regular visits to the Head Office in Milan. They were wonderful employers and very easy to work with.

Veglia and Borletti were two Italian suppliers of car parts who started producing different gauges at the beginning of the 20th Century. For the automobile industry, they mainly produced clocks, tachometers, speedometers, oil pressure gauges, battery gauges and any instrument to measure something. Even though the products were mainly designed to use in sport cars, they were also used on bikes like Vespa and even on racing boats.

The Borletti brothers founded the company in 1897 in Milan in order to produce licensed watches - American, Swiss and German. The company was transformed for military purposes during World War I to then become a manufacturer of precision mechanisms in the aftermath. Borletti acquired the brand Veglia on July 15th 1930. Veglia was the brand used by Fratelli Borletti to produce kitchenware, clocks and other fine instruments.

At the time the company was producing gauges on a stand-alone basis they supplied to other non-Italian car manufacturers like Mercedes-Benz for their racing cars. The German automaker used them until 1950. Italian carmakers had used them too for decades.
Magneti Marelli acquired Veglia Borletti in 1987.

George though had hankered much to have his own business and in 1963 he left Borletti Veglia to open his first retail outlet in Croydon. This was a sewing centre where he sold sewing and knitting machines, fabric, haberdashery and similar. Specialist staff undertook repairs to the machines, both domestic and industrial and contracts were obtained for machine maintenance in schools, hospitals and factories. Further shops were opened in Sittingbourne, Maidstone and two further in the Medway Towns.

The business flourished but the death of Eileen in January 1995 affected George deeply. Despite the buzz experienced through owning your own business, George gradually lost interest and in 1998 closed the business altogether and retired from gainful employment.

George and Eileen

When at school, George met Eileen on the Number 63 Bus that went from Horsham Railway Station to Wisborough Green. They both used the same bus frequently. On one occasion there was a bet between George and a number of his school friends to take Eileen out to the pictures – Eileen's mother, Edith, was held in high dread and would be an obstacle of sorts to overcome or get around before any date could be effected. George accepted the bet and won in so far as he took Eileen out on date.

The venue was the Odeon Cinema in Horsham – the site now occupied by Sun Life. The Cinema in North Street, Horsham was designed in the Art Deco Style by George Coles [1884 – 1963]. It opened on Wednesday October 7th, 1936 being built at a cost of £33,555. It could accommodate 1,258 patrons. It closed as an Odeon in 1967 and was taken over by Classic. The cinema closed in 1976. The building was demolished by November 1981 for an office block occupied by Sun Life Assurance.

The Odeon, Horsham, then and now – much changed!

The Art Deco building replaced by the functional metal and glass.

The romance continued through the War Years and continued after the War and again George resumed the relationship once 'demobbed'. The Odeon Cinema featured on one of the more memorable occasions.

That Saturday, November 29th, 1947, Horsham Town were playing Northampton Town in the 1st Round of the F.A. Cup. On the way into the cinema the local newspaper billboards were reporting that Horsham had sensationally taken the lead and were a goal up – the score line being 1 – 0. On leaving the cinema George noted that the same billboards had now the depressing news for local readers that the final score was 9 - 1 in favour of Northampton Town.

No progress was made beyond the first qualifying round stage until season 1937/38 when the club bucked that trend in surprising style, going all the way through to the fourth and final qualifying round before being knocked out in a replay by Enfield, thus denying us a tie against Bristol City. A decade later, Horsham created history when reaching the first round of the competition proper. Victory over Redhill, in front of over 5,500 spectators, was rewarded with a trip to then Third Division side Notts County, a club that had just created shockwaves by signing former Everton, Chelsea and England striker Tommy Lawton for a then record fee of £20,000. Yet Horsham stunned the near 29,000 crowd by taking a second minute lead through Ron Smallwood, only for the professionals to stage a stunning recovery in which Lawton scored three of his new side's nine goals. Though no disgrace, this remains Horsham's heaviest defeat in the competition.

Notts County 9   *Horsham 1*
Lawton [3], Sewell [3] marsh [2] Freeman   *Smallwood*

Nottingham suffered a minor invasion as Horsham supporters flooded into the town by coach, rail and car wearing Lincoln green and amber favours and headed for the Meadow Lane ground. Undaunted by the formidable task that faced their team and the arduous journey of one hundred and seventy miles, they streamed into the ground at least an hour before the kick-off. Many of the women wore bonnets of crepe paper in green and amber, while Mrs. Maggie Woods sported a complete outfit in the town colours.

Almost completely filling the two end blocks of the stand, Horsham fans roared out 'Sussex by the Sea' in opposition to the band on the pitch until they complied by play-ing the tune for them. George Cutler earned a roar when he paraded round the touch-line resplendent in a green and amber top hat and bearing a miniature FA Cup and green and amber umbrella, solemnly doffing his topper to the delighted crowd. He earned another burst of cheering when he danced a waltz in the centre of the pitch with Mrs. Woods and then scored a goal after some tricky footwork with an imaginary ball.

Complete families had made the trip and Mr. and Mrs. Goacher of Park Street even brought their retriever, Rex, who attended all of Horsham's games. Two other specta-tors were Tom Waller, a Horsham supporter who was blinded in World War One, and his companion Bill Luxford who, after twenty-five years in the Royal Navy, lost his leg in the last week of World War Two. Bill provided a running commentary on the match for Tom.

The huge contingent of Horsham supporters got their reward when their team scored a picture goal after just two minutes' play. Notts County kicked off and Horsham straightaway gained possession and started a series of rapid thrusts that startled the County defence by their cohesion and speed. Bob Hughes whipped the ball away from a County forward and put a pass down the middle to Den Daubney. The centre-forward made ground before flicking the ball to Snowy Roberts who slipped it forward to Ron Smallwood. The winger passed back to his inside man and dashed into the middle to meet a perfect centre just inside the penalty area and he sent the ball crashing into the top of the net with a powerful left-foot drive.

For the next fifteen minutes Horsham held grimly to their lead, with Hughes and Roy Lindfield frequently getting the better of their duels with England international, Tommy Lawton. But then Sewell drew Hughes out of position before centring to an unmarked Lawton who equalised from close range. Charlie Hemsley had a glorious chance to restore Horsham's lead a few minutes later when another good movement on the right wing ended with the ball arriving at his feet in front of goal but he only managed to balloon his shot over the bar. Horsham held on tenaciously but then the County wing-halves got a grip on the game and two quick goals in the thirtieth and thirty-first minutes put the home team in a winning position. Lawton sent Marsh away and the inside-left put in a low shot. George Power dived a little too soon and the greasy ball flew into the goal over his body. Lawton added number three with a snap shot taken on the turn twenty-five yards out.

To be only 3-1 down at half-time was a great credit to Horsham and it was not until an hour had passed that County improved on their lead. The early minutes of the second half again saw Horsham on the attack and Smallwood made Brown double back quickly to hold a dropping shot. The Sussex side appealed strongly for a penalty for hands which appeared to be justified, but the referee waved play on. That was the last serious challenge from the Horsham forwards before the inevitable superiority and speed of the professionals began to tell and they added six more goals through Lawton, Sewell (3), Marsh and Freeman. The last goal came only two minutes from full-time. Hughes held Lawton well, but the inside-forwards were so active that he was often forced to leave the centre-forward in order to cover the inside men. Nevertheless, it was a remarkable feature that all Lawton's goals were scored with his feet and not one with his 'special' headers.

Power in goal earned roars of applause for his many spectacular saves and he had little chance with any of the second half goals. Owen Parker played at the top of his form at right-half, working untiringly and not being frightened of holding the ball to beat his man before sending it forward. Lindfield several times outstripped Lawton for speed and kept Cumnor, the international left winger, remarkably subdued. Smallwood was the pick of the forwards, and was a constant menace on the right wing while John Ripley played a real captain's role at inside-left and found his long experience helping him against the professionals.

It was a tribute to the amateurs that only a handful of the 24,815 spectators left the ground before the final whistle and that they rose as one man to cheer the Horsham players as they left the field battered and leg-weary but still undaunted.
– website of Horsham Town Football Club.

Eileen and George were married in St Peter Ad Ancula Church, Wisborough Green on January 1st, 1949. George's best man was Len Higgins; the two had served together for much of the war – all of the War in fact except for the last three months in the Far East!

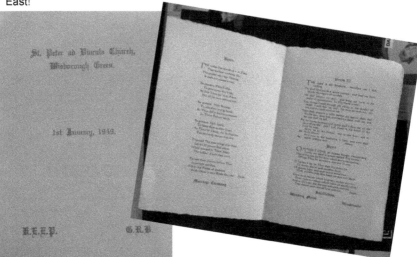

The earliest documents so far found which mention St Peter Ad Ancula Church are both dated 1227, the eleventh year of the reign of Henry III. One is a grant by the King to the Archdeacon of Lewes to hold a yearly fair on the vigil day and morrow of St Peter ad Vincula and a market day weekly on Thursday at Wyseberg. The other is a reference in the Bishop's Register stating that the living of Wisborough, formerly part of the prebend of Aldingbourne, was to

be a prebend by itself. A prebendal stall of Wisborough is still in Chichester Cathedral. The name Wisborough is probably derived from the Saxon words 'wisc' a river meadow and 'beorg' a hill. The village was sometimes just called 'Green'. The dedication of the Church is mentioned in several wills of different dates. For instance, in 1520 William Phylippe directed his body 'to be buryed and enthird in the church yarde of Sainte Peter and Sainte Paule called Grene' and willed '13s 4d be spent at my burying in all charges whereof I will have V masses of the V woundes and every priest to have 6d'. The registers begin in the reign of Elizabeth I, and are kept now at the Diocesan Records Office in Chichester. The list of vicars begins in 1273 and can be seen beside the south door. The church has no monuments older than 1667 and their inscriptions are all clear.

The western end of the nave, with its herringbone masonry and Norman doors and windows, is the earliest part of the present building, although there was probably a Saxon church before. The hilltop site and unusually thick walls (4' 6") suggest that for a time it was a Norman keep guarding the upper reaches of the river Arun which was an important means of transport when the Weald was thickly forested. It is certainly odd that the west door, normally the main entrance to a church, is not central and is so much smaller than the north and south doors which were built high enough to admit mounted men. By the time of Henry I, the building was again a church extending eastwards to the chancel arch, but with a lower roof and probably a small apse at the east end. The chancel arch was narrower than at present and flanked by two arched recesses against which the nave altars would have been set. The south recess with its medieval painting can still be seen. The slab of Petworth marble set in the northwest corner of the chancel floor is thought to be one of the nave altar stones. The aisles were added in the 13th century, possibly in the reign of Henry III, a great age for church building, and have been altered at various later dates. The font dates from the same period. The nave roof was raised in the 14th century and clerestory windows inserted. At around the same time the tower was built within the southwest corner, probably because the hill site was very restricted. Last to be added (apart from the brick buttresses of 1838) were two porches in the 15th century.

The chancel was built in the 13th Century in Early English style, with lancet windows in which the stained glass is Victorian. The altar is the original stone one from before the Reformation, when Henry VIII ordered all stone altars to be destroyed and replaced with wooden tables. - However, parishioners arranged to hide the altar in a new vicarage being built in Loxwood - as the chimney breast! The King's Commissioners were apparently satisfied that the altar had been broken up. It returned to Wisborough Green in 1901 when the Loxwood vicarage was demolished and was stored on church land pending a decision about its future. It was not replaced in the chancel then, as at that time stone altars were still somewhat frowned upon as being Papist. Thirty years later it was decided to do the work, setting the altar on a base found by Mr Arthur Penfold Wyatt, churchwarden. The stonemasons, who had dressed the base because of a misunderstanding, were luckily stopped before they did the top, as the consecration crosses could still just be seen. The work was finished in 1937 as a memorial to Mr Wyatt.

The newly married couple managed to acquire a small flat in Kensington. Accommodation was scarce at the time due to the wartime bombing. The flat left a lot to be desired but it was home and there was a front door. Money was also tight but the newly weds managed with the main consolation being that they were blissfully happy. They had survived the War with the sole source of communication being by letter or card. They always felt that if they survived the War that the loss of Eileen's father when she was just 14 they could survive anything.

The first present George bought Eileen after their marriage was Paddy, a Cocker Spaniel. It did cost near three weeks' pay. The dog was their entertainment and pastime all rolled into one. They spent hours in Kensington Gardens, Hyde Park, Putney Towpath and Wimbledon Common taking her for walks. At weekends it was window shopping in Knightsbridge, Kensington and Sloane Square. They were truly contented after the previous six years of deprivation.

The family with George's mother Mary on left, and, front row from left to right Linda and Paddy.

Linda, the centre of attention with George on right and George's father William on left. The family dog is again in the picture!

Paddy was no ordinary Cocker Spaniel – she was the granddaughter of Tracey Witch of Ware. Tracey Witch of Ware won the title of Best In Show at Cruft's in both 1948 and 1950. She missed out on the Best in Show judging in 1952 because of a delay in breed judging, and also became Reserve Best in Show in 1953. Tracey Witch was bred by Denise Weldon from the sire Falconers Padlock of Ware and the dam Whist. She was a descendent of the previous Cruft's Best in Show winner Luckystar of Ware and Reserve Best in Show winner Whoopee of Ware. Tracey Witch was subsequently purchased by H. S. Lloyd, owner of the "of Ware" kennels.

Following the Second World War, Cruft's resumed in 1948. At the time there was a Reserve Best in Show named for each of the two days of competition with the winner of the first day going forward to compete once more on the second day. Tracey Witch was named the best of the dogs shown on the second day and faced the Wire Fox Terrier Drakehall Dairymaid for the title of Best in Show. Judges May Pacey and Arthur Coxton Smith awarded the title to Tracey Witch. Such was the rush of the crowds to congratulate owner Bert Lloyd, that Tracey Witch was given a police escort.

There had been no event run in 1949 as the date changed from October to February in 1950. In 1950, she again won the breed class and the Sporting Group, and was once more named Best in Show.] In 1951, she lost in the Best of Breed, defeated by fellow "of Ware" dog, Joywyns Blueboy of Ware. The following year she won the Best of Breed title once again, but by the time the judging was completed for the English Cocker Spaniels, Best in Show had already been judged and awarded to the Bulldog, Ch. Noways Chuckles. This resulted in several protests from the spectators, and the Cruft's officials attempted to find a solution but couldn't find a way for Tracey Witch to face Noways Chuckles in the ring.

In 1953, she returned to Cruft's once more at the age of eight. She again won Best of Breed, and the Gundog Group. Tracey Witch was awarded reserve overall for the first day, with the Great Dane Ch. Elch Elder of Ouborough named as the victor on each of the two days and awarded the title of Best in Show. During the course of her career, Tracey Witch of Ware won a total of 52 challenge certificates. She was H. S. Lloyds' most successful dog, having won Best in Show on thirteen occasions at all-breed championship shows.

On September 2nd, 1951 George and Eileen were blessed with the arrival of their daughter, Linda. The couple had decided that if the new baby were a boy then he would be Patrick Ian [covering the Celtic Nations] and if a girl, either Linda or Anne. They were pleased and proud – life was now complete. George has many happy memories of taking the newly born out in the pram in Kensington Gardens. He felt everyone was looking at him in admiration. Such is the life of a father with a newly born!

Linda in time grew up and was to pass the 11 Plus. She obtained a place at Woodford High School for Girls. After one term there the family moved to Maidstone. Linda transferred to Maidstone High School for Girls. The family quickly settled in Barming and George is still living in the same house 56 years later! Eileen worked for Age Concern and was a Councillor, representing the Heat Ward, with Maidstone Council. She died on January 3rd, 1995.

Linda initially went to St Mary Hospital, Paddington to train as a physiotherapist. However, she found the training unrewarding so subsequently went to the West London College and qualified as a Medical Secretary.

Linda married Andrew Barbour in November 1982 at St Margaret of Antioch Church, Barming.

On qualifying she worked in London but then secured a position in Hong Kong where she spent seven years. It was here she met her future husband Andrew Barbour.

The couple married in the local Church in Barming, St Margaret of Antioch, in November 1982. The family lived in Taunton, Somerset until 1994 when they moved to Cheshire. They have two sons Edward and Christopher. Edward works as TV sound engineer in Manchester. Chris is Deputy Manager of a pupil referral unit in Liverpool. Despite the distance the family remains close and tight knit.

Chapter 5 - The Veteran

On his own and in retirement George had to occupy himself. It was not long before his local Church were about to form a charity, the Friends of Barming Church. The charity was created to raise money for the upkeep of the Church. George was asked to be treasurer. It turned out to be really interesting and required some input from all of the Committee members. The work was covered by so many regulations that that in itself was an all-consuming job.

In 1798 Edmund Hasted, Kent historian, wrote of the St Margaret of Antioch Church, *standing by itself among a grove of elms, the slight, delicate spire rising above the foliage of the grove, affords a pleasing prospect.*

Barming people have worshipped and have ma-rked the most important events in their lives here for nearly 900 years. The original church was built around 1120, no doubt on the orders of the powerful de Clare family who had been Lords of the Manor of East Barming since the Norman Conquest. There was no village then - just a scattering of maybe 30 peasant families - and the church would have been built next to the manor house. West Barming ("Little Barming", now Barnjet) was a separate manor and had its own church, but by the late 1400s it had fallen into ruins. Some say St Margaret's stands on the site of a Roman villa.

It seems to have been built on a solid stone base and Roman remains, including some elaborate stone coffins, were found near the church in the 19th century. There is no mention of an East or West Barming church in the Domesday Book and no physical trace of a Saxon church, but Augustine began his work in Kent in 597 and Rochester Cathedral was dedicated in 604, so we can be sure there was a Christian community here long before St Margaret's. Like all country churches, St Margaret's has changed as a building. It was upgraded with a tower and porch in the prosperous 1400s, stripped during the Reformation, and drastically restored by the Victorians, but its essential character has not changed. It remains what it has always been: an unpretentious and welcoming church, especially for local people.

So with the Committee's help fundraising started. It was all the usual local village events but over £100,000 was raised. In due course George became Chairman of the Friends. However, as George became involved in Veteran matters he had less time to work with the local committee.

In 1997 George received a telephone call with some sad news. His great friend, Len Higgins, who hailed from Hereford and with whom George had joined the Army with in 1943 was seriously ill in hospital in Hereford. George immediately drove to Hereford and spent a few days with him at his home. A week later, and back in Barming, George had a 'phone call from Len's son to say that his father had died. In the course of conversation when with Len he asked George if he were a member of the Normandy Veterans' Association. Len's immediate advice was to join the Association.

After attending Len's funeral George felt he owed if to Len to join. Encountering the usual difficulties of information on how and where to join, George eventually became a member of South East Branch, Number 23. In 1999 the Branch Secretary was taken ill and George was requested to replace him. He immediately found the work interesting. Dealing with the day to day running., organising the various visits, arranging an annual visit to Normandy for D-Day Commemorations was in some senses fulfilling.

Normandy Veterans Annual Parade at the Cenotaph, Whitehall; June 10th, 2007

South East Branch, Number 23 Chairman Vic Longhurst, centre.

In 1981 in Cleethorpes on the Humber Estuary in Lincolnshire, four Normandy Veterans created the impetus that would morph into the Normandy Veterans Association. The Association would grow to 105 Branches with representation in Australia, Belgium, Canada, France, Holland and Ireland with a membership exceeding 15,000. This gradually progressed to members attending Parades and Services in many places in the U.K., Belgium, France and Holland.

Like all Regimental Associations, the tradition of having a standard for Parade, was adopted, one being designed. Eventually every Branch on formation were obliged to have their own standard with the same design as the original but with the name of the

Branch and number. This then was paraded at local and national events. This was quite a sight to behold at National events with upwards of 80 – 90 Standards on parade and several thousand Veterans marching behind.

Besides the Parade and Service at Colleville-Montgomery during the yearly pilgrimage undertaken by the Branch the visit to Bayeux Cathedral and Cemetery was always made. Arromanches and Jerusalem Cemetery were other venues, but other Cemeteries and sites were also visited at Branch members' requests. The days were always spent in Remembrance.

The Branch organised collections at various times of the year which invariably proved a success. 'H' Jeal always attracted a crowd in Gravesend when he was collecting – having served with the Black Watch he wore a kilt with great pride. He had followed the tradition with the Regiment as his father had also served with the Black Watch in World War 1.

In 2004 the National Committee of the Normandy Veterans' Association had a severe blow. Within three months, the National Chairman, the National Secretary and the National Treasurer all died. This was a difficult and problematic position for the Association bearing in mind that there were in excess of 14,000 members. George was asked if he would stand as National Treasurer to which he readily agreed. It was quite an honour and once he had the accounts sorted out and on a good footing and everything was running smoothly George was embarking on another career!

On the 65th Anniversary of D-Day in June 2009 the National Secretary resigned and George was appointed to the post, he now held two of the most important positions in the Association. This meant many hours of work a day as he was now dealing with all

Juno Beach; meeting up with Canadian Royal Engineers Veterans!!

National events in the country and in Normandy. It meant contacting and meeting many people, organising and attending regular committee meetings and official visits to all sorts of events and organisations.

Besides the annual June visit to Normandy there were other notable events in the yearly calendar. The annual Parade and Service at the Cenotaph, Whitehall at the end of June was foremost. This was invariably a huge occasion and every Branch was represented. The Brigade of Guards Band led the march past and furnished the music for the Service. In addition to the many Veterans there were the countless family support and other well-wishers.

As is always the case, the event came to an end. The Band of the Irish Guards was in attendance for the final reunion. The Band completed their programme with *Wish Me Luck as You Wave Me Goodbye* followed by *Old Lang Syne* – a most moving finale. It was an occasion never to be forgotten and is still talked of by those who were there at the time.

The other major occasions the Normandy Veterans attended include of course the National Service of Remembrance or, failing that, attending their own local Service of Remembrance. There was also the annual Service in York Minster.

another tour – to Ieper; enjoying a welcome break and drink at Hill 62…

…Remembrance at Thiepval; David Greig with the bugle.

Work with Schools

George has over the years visited countless schools and has become, for some, an extra member of staff. Whether it is visiting schools or accompanying students on tours George has proven to be very popular. His circuit varies from Canterbury to Sevenoaks and from Maidstone to Gravesend. George caters for all age groups and is equally at home in a Primary School as he is talking to 6th Form Students. He has also been the Guest of Honour at various events from Prize Giving to History Days.

Berlin, 2006 with one of the local bears and 6th Form students of St John's Catholic School, Gravesend.

Tours to Normandy are of particular interest to and relevance for George.

George is seen here with Madame Arlette Gondrée-Pritchett, having arranged the meeting with students at the Café Gondrée.

School Tour, 2012.

Normandy Tour, June 2010; 20 students from St John's Catholic School, Gravesend and 20 veterans of the Normandy Campaign – quite an experience.

George was very involved with the Imperial War Museum and *Their Past Your Future* project. The work included visiting schools and George was the lead in what became known in the North Kent area as the 'four musketeers' – the four being 'H' Jeal, John Roberts, Joe Hoadley and George. The four would visit a school and literally take over any assembly or classroom through their presence and dignity. Students vied to hear them speak. Unfortunately, the years have taken the toll of the 'four musketeers' and George is now the sole survivor.

This has not diminished George's enthusiasm nor interest in visiting schools and speaking to students.

Three of the Four Musketeers –
From left, John Roberts, Joe Hoadley and 'H' Jeal.

Bayeux Cemetery – George with Joe on his right and John on his left.

Another talk – George delivering with John and 'H' seated, listening.

The Interviews

It was on a school tour with students of St John's, Gravesend that George and the Head of History at the school conceived the idea of interviewing Normandy Veterans. On that tour some 10 Veterans of the Normandy Campaign joined 20 6th Form students on a uniquely educational tour spread over five days. The plan was to undertake the interviews at uniquely relevant points – thus Harry Card was interviewed at Hermanville where on June 6th, *HMS Swift* was anchored, being one of the ships that commenced the bombardment. John Roberts was interviewed where he landed with the 2nd East Yorkshires and George was interviewed on the beach at Asnelles where he came ashore.

Interviewed in Dartford in June, 2013 – from left, Ian Hammerton, George, Jim Radford and George Dangerfield.

Back in Kent and at a meeting of the South East Branch, N.V.A., George developed the concept further and eleven members were interviewed. The idea developed further with Brigadier Clive Elderton conducting interviews the length and breadth of the country. By the time the Brigadier had completed his tour he had interviewed over 160 Normandy veterans during 2013 and 2014. Five interviews were undertaken at St John's School with Harry Card and Joe Hoadley among the group.

The Heritage Lottery Fund made a grant to *Legasee* and the NVA for putting 100 of the interviews online, and producing educational resources for schools that make use of the interviews. St John's School was one of the two schools that carried out a pilot programme on the educational resources on an History Day at the school in 2015.

On the 2012 St John's School tour – George, above, signing the Dakota at the C47-Café, Ste Mère Église and looking over the area of Sword Beach at Asnelles where he landed on June 6th, 1944 prior to standing in front of the camera for an interview!

Awards and Recognition of George's work

On June 6th, 2009 George was invited to receive the **Legion d'Honneur** in recognition of his work with the Normandy Veterans' Association

The *Ordre National de la Légion d'Honneur* - The Legion of Honour (National Order of the Legion of Honour) - is the highest French order of merit for military and civil merits, established in 1802 by Napoleon Bonaparte and retained by all later French governments and régimes. The order's motto is *Honneur et Patrie* ("Honour and Fatherland"), and its seat is the Palais de la Légion d'Honneur next to the Musée d'Orsay, on the left bank of the Seine in Paris.

While membership in the *Légion* is technically restricted to French nationals, foreign nationals who have served France or the ideals it upholds may receive the honour. Foreign nationals who live in France are subject to the same requirements as the French. Foreign nationals who live abroad may be awarded a distinction of any rank or dignity in the *Légion*. Foreign heads of state and their spouses or consorts of monarchs are made Grand Cross as a courtesy. American and British veterans who served in either World War I on French soil, or during the 1944 campaigns to liberate France, may be eligible for appointment as Chevalier of the Legion of Honour, provided they were still living when the honour was approved.

George with his escort on the occasion of the award in Paris.

George became a Knight of the Legion d'Honneur at a ceremony marking the 65th anniversary of D-Day. He was presented with the Chevalier medal by the French minister of state for defence and veterans, Jean-Marie Bockel.

RÉPUBLIQUE FRANÇAISE

MINISTÈRE DE LA DÉFENSE

Le Ministre

07 OCT 09 – 014085
Paris, le
N° /DEF/CAB/CM 11/PREST
Ct: 2009

Monsieur,

Le 5 juin 2009, alors que nous nous apprêtions à commémorer le 65ème anniversaire du débarquement de Normandie, j'ai mesuré l'honneur qui m'était fait de pouvoir vous remettre au nom de M. Nicolas Sarkozy, Président de la République et en présence du chef d'état major des armées, dans la cour d'honneur de l'hôtel national des invalides, la croix de la légion d'honneur.

En vous décorant de la plus haute distinction de notre République, la France a voulu se souvenir avec émotion du sacrifice suprême consenti par vos compagnons d'armes pour la défense des valeurs de liberté et la destruction de toutes les formes de barbarie. Grâce à vos actions exemplaires, à votre héroïsme et à votre engagement en faveur de la liberté, vous avez aidé la France à se relever et à retrouver son honneur. La France n'oubliera jamais.

Afin que cette cérémonie ne devienne pas qu'un souvenir, j'ai voulu faire réaliser un film, véritable témoignage de cet instant unique et solennel. Il m'est très agréable de pouvoir vous l'adresser aujourd'hui.

En espérant très sincèrement que vous pourrez savourer ces instants avec une légitime fierté en compagnie de vos proches et en vous assurant à nouveau de toute la reconnaissance de la France, je vous prie d'agréer, Monsieur, l'assurance de ma considération distinguée.

Très cordialement

Hervé MORIN

Mr. George Robert BATTS

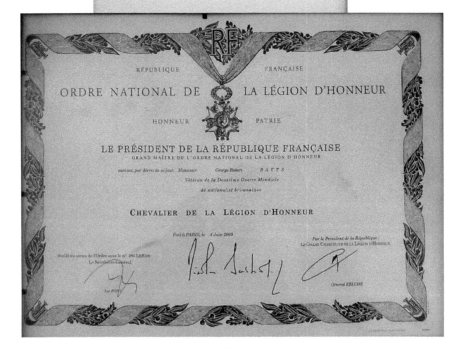

118

Five years later came recognition closer to home. George received the **Point of Light Award** on June 6th, 2014 by the then Prime Minister, the Rt Hon David Cameron. The Award was made in recognition of George's work with the Normandy Veterans' Association.

Points of Light are outstanding individual volunteers – people who are making a change in their community.

First established by President George H. W. Bush in 1990, over 6,000 US Points of Light have been recognised in the USA. UK Points of Light was developed in partnership with the US programme and launched in the Cabinet Room at 10 Downing Street in April 2014.

The Points of Light highlight an enormous array of innovative and inspirational volunteering across the length and breadth of Britain. Doing everything from tackling knife crime, to supporting families of dementia patients, our UK Points of Light are fundraising, awareness raising, problem solving heroes who all had an idea they decided to make a reality.

Their actions have changed lives and their stories can inspire thousands more to get involved or start their own initiatives.

Points of Lights / 10 Downing Street/Prime Minister's Office website [https://www.pointsoflight.gov.uk]

1O DOWNING STREET
LONDON SW1A 2AA

6 June 2014

Dear George,

Congratulations!

I am delighted to be recognising you as the thirty-seventh UK Point of Light.

UK Points of Light is a new award which recognises outstanding individual volunteers - points of light in our country - who are doing extraordinary things in the service of others.

You have spent decades volunteering to ensure that no-one forgets the sacrifice your generation made for our freedom. As Honorary Secretary of the Normandy Veterans Association you have played a key role in arranging the annual trips to the beaches of Northern France. The DVD you are creating with interviews with 200 veterans will ensure there is a lasting account of that historic day for generations to come.

I believe it is my duty as Prime Minister to hold up examples of great volunteering and service as an inspiration to others. Through your hard work and dedication you are making our communities stronger, and our country a better place.

On behalf of the whole country, I hope this Points of Light Award can be a small way of saying thank you.

With all good wishes —

Yours,

David

George Batts

D-Day veteran leading commemoration
37. George Batts

A D-Day veteran who for decades has given up his free time to ensure that others remember the sacrifice that his generation made.

Despite being 88, George Batts from Kent gives up a considerable amount of his own time volunteering for the Normandy Veterans Association (NVA). He is the current Honorary Secretary and plays a key role in organising the annual trips to the beaches of northern France.

Over 70 years ago, George joined the army aged seventeen and trained as a Royal Engineer. After weeks of rumoured action in Europe his unit were taken to a base on the South Coast. When they were each given a handful of Francs, they knew where they were heading. In the early hours of June 6th 1944, George landed on Gold Beach and became part of the liberation of France. George remembers incredible noise, the navy bombarding the coast, planes overhead and paratroopers dropping from the sky. Recognising that he was a part of a historical moment, George has dedicated much of his life to ensure memories of the day continue to be shared and that the fallen are not forgotten.

George refers to the Normandy visits as a 'pilgrimage' to honour those who lost their lives. Through the NVA, each year George helps veterans to make a pilgrimage to Normandy. Whilst in France, George arranges visits to the cemeteries for veterans to pay respect to their fallen comrades. He has even advised the MOD on this year's 70th anniversary commemorative events, in particular the Bayeux Cemetery Service and the ceremony at Arromanches that the Queen along with other members of the Royal Family are due to attend.

Away from Normandy, George has delivered countless conferences, talks and presentations to school groups, recounting his experiences of D-Day. In order to create a lasting account of World War Two, George is helping to create a DVD with interviews of 200 veterans which will form part of the exhibitions at the D-Day museum in Portsmouth. Being the 70th anniversary of D-Day, this year's ceremony is all the more important, especially as the NVA are finally set to disband at the end of this year. Thanks to their and George's efforts the soldiers, sailors and airmen who paid the ultimate sacrifice in WW2 will be remembered by future generations.

Prime Minister David Cameron said:
"Seventy years on we look back on D-Day and the heroes, like George, who risked their lives for this country. George's continued efforts over the years to educate others and remind us all of what happened on that important day in history are remarkable and I'm delighted to recognise him as a Point of Light."

Points of Lights / 10 Downing Street/Prime Minister's Office website
[https://www.pointsoflight.gov.uk]

Following on from his meeting with David Cameron George suggested the building of a Memorial to those who died under British Command during the Normandy Campaign, there being none. The Prime Minster immediately supported the proposal and money was allocated for the project. George is currently the Patron of the *Normandy Memorial Trust.*

POINTS
OF LIGHT

PRESENTED TO

George Batts

In recognition of your outstanding volunteering

Signed
Rt Hon David Cameron MP Prime Minister

10 DOWNING STREET
LONDON SW1A 2AA

George was included in the New Year's Honours List in January 2016. He received his **_M.B.E._** for his work with the Normandy Veterans' Association, Veterans generally and his work in Education. The Investiture was on March 1st at Buckingham Palace. George remembers how thrilled he was when he received the M.B.E from the Queen herself.

George and his daughter Linda after the Investiture.

Letters of support for the M.B.E. were quickly forthcoming and from a variety of sources -

July 17ᵗʰ, 2014   St John's Catholic School, Gravesend

Ref; Mr George Batts, Légion d'Honneur
Back in May, 2004 St John's Catholic School won the inaugural Their Past Your Future prize of a five day tour of Normandy. The Their Past Your Future event was sponsored, operated under the control of the Imperial War Museum. George Batts was one of four Normandy Veterans who visited the school on the occasion of the prize giving. This was the Schools' introduction to George and without hesitation it was immediately evident that George would have an everlasting impact on the school.
In the decade since, George has been a constant visitor to the school and has accompanied us on numerous school tours; he has mentored students both from

the school and from visiting schools; he has spoken to assemblies, large and small at the school and has been an important ambassador for St John's.

The students have benefitted enormously through George's invitation to such events as Trooping the Colours, Remembrance Day at the Cenotaph, the Normandy Veterans' Remembrance at the Cenotaph, various events at Horse Guards' Parade and at St Paul's Cathedral. George has also been instrumental in St John's presence at various and many events in the Gravesham and Rochester areas.

George remains ever enthusiastic in coming to school and meeting and talking to students. He is a regular at such events as our History Day and Remembrance and Holocaust Assemblies. He speaks with clarity, sympathy and empathy and in a language that not alone engages the students but is readily understood by all. He speaks with sincerity and from the heart.

When his services are called on George will readily answer. He not alone ensures his presence but also the presence of members of the local Normandy Veterans' Association Branch. He was instrumental in ensuring a good number of veterans when St John's was host to our very first school group visit from abroad – Lorentz Lyceum, Arnhem. The visitors were overwhelmed to have speakers who were familiar with Arnhem! George ensured we had no less than eight veterans on the return visit to Arnhem.

George has been a regular on the school tours to Normandy which now number five in all. He will be present again as our guest next year when the school visits Normandy in early April, 2015. He has also been on the three visits to Berlin and Krakow. George ensures a diplomatic tone at all times and, although a veteran, he is warmly received wherever he goes to include Germany. He remains unruffled, ever calm and has a calming effect on both students and staff even in the most trying circumstance.

George is also a regular on the school battlefield Tours to the Somme and to Ypres and despite the early start/late return and the time of year [late Autumn and winter] he is an ever present feature giving guidance and advice to staff and student but not beyond taking on the role of staff himself. He is ever supportive and readily gives of his profound and substantive knowledge of tour organising.

George is an excellent worker and organiser. It is a tremendous privilege to work with him, making the various plans. He readily pours over any documentation, reading the small print and ensuring all contingency situations are covered. He himself has instigated a number of veteran/student tours – Duxford Air Show, the Imperial War Museum and other events in London come immediately to mind. George has also been very much involved in the planning, organising and management of such school events as the annual war time music show, History Day, the LIFE AT THE SHARP END series of paperback books [reminiscences of veterans published in book format – 200/300 pages] and the CD of War Time music and the concert that followed that launched the CD.

George has proved an inspiration to staff and students and has ensured that the numbers studying history at GCSE and A level have increased as well those studying history at University level. Many past pupils remember him fondly and remain in contact with him such is his influence on them. There are far too many events and celebrations and commemorations to numerate; all one can add is that whenever he is available [which is 100%] he will be present. It is demeaning to make a list or a count George is so well known in the school that he is regarded as another member of staff.

He is ever welcome and open; when travelling to Portsmouth in May to see Alistair Dutch and George introduce the Normandy Veterans' Association programme of interviewing veterans of the Normandy Campaign, George was the first person to be met and seen, with his arms open and a broad welcoming smile and greeting.

It is not wonder then that George will lead the talks on the History Induction Day on September 9th, 2015; there he will be leading two talks – one to students who have taken up GCSE as a subject and one to the A Level students. He is ever in demand and will also be figuring in the approaching Careers' Day when various speakers will be in school to motivate the students. His talks are such that every student listens intently to what he says. He will also be engaged with the R.E. Department adding to their speakers on such themes as the just war and religion and war.

George is a devout individual and this contributes in no small way to his assimilation into a Faith School.

George has become a personal friend of mine; he has an 'open house' whereby I may come and go at any time to avail of his expertise and friendship.

He has ensured my continuing enthusiasm as a teacher of history and has ensured my continued study into 20th Century History and in particular has added enormously to my understanding of the D-Day Campaign. Standing on Gold Beach with George remains one of the highlights of my life; recounting his time in Normandy in the summer of 1944. What is more remarkable is that his account remains full of humour with fascinating incidents being given a humorous twist.

George has an infectious sense of humour and treats life the way it should be treated – head on and with a smile. He is a rather modest person who would be overwhelmed if he discovers he has been nominated for an award never mind actually being granted one. On the occasion of the Légion d'Honneur he repeatedly asked me whether he was deserving of such an award!

One could write a book on George and there are plans, not that he is aware of this at the moment, that the school History Society will do so. He thoroughly deserves any accolade coming to him. I have only touched on his contribution to the school and his effect on me; nothing has been mentioned of the fact that his contribution to life at St John's is in extra to his other commitments – to other schools and

to the Normandy Veterans' Association. He is a workaholic but his work is to the betterment of everyone he comes in contact with.
A thoroughly excellent individual in every sense.
Colm Murphy
Head of History & Head of House

To whom it may concern...

It gives me great pleasure to be able to endorse such a great man to be able to receive what I consider to be long overdue recognition by his country.

George Batts is more than a war hero, he is one of the most inspirational men I have ever met. Despite his age, George works indefatigably with numerous contrasting groups to ensure that one of our nation's greatest achievements is never forgotten.

George's work with schools, museums, local and national media are at the forefront of national remembrance whilst his work with his fellow veterans ensure that those who were actually on the front line of the Second World War continue their process of counselling with their contemporaries - an important factor, often overlooked and a factor which was shamelessly lacking at the time of their return home from war almost seven decades ago.

In short George is an inspiration to all he meets. He is nothing short of a national treasure and I believe him worthy of any honour bestowed upon him by his nation.

Sincerely...

Stuart M. Robertson BA(Hons)
Historian, Author and Full Time Battlefield Guide.
1 Le Port
50480
Neuville au Plain
FRANCE

Letters of congratulations were equally as abundant -

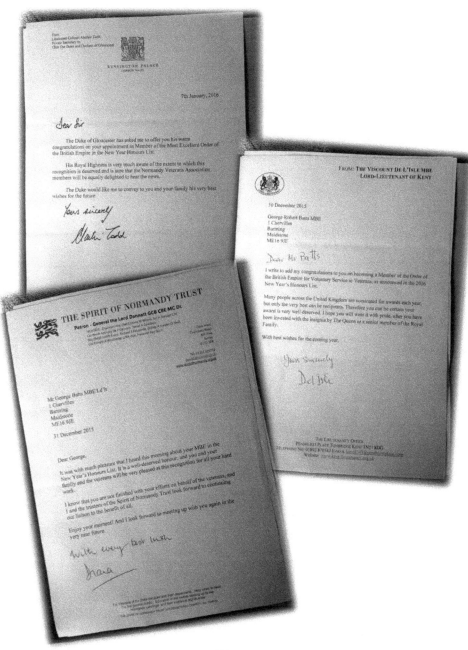

LAYING UP THE STANDARD OF THE SOUTH EAST BRANCH, NORMANDY VETERANS' ASSOCIATION

The standard of South East Branch, Normandy Veterans' Association was laid up in April 2018. It was decided to celebrate the close association that the Branch had with Colleville-Montgomery and with Chouain that both would feature in the service of the laying down of the standard.

A 45 strong group to include three Veterans of the Normandy Campaign attended the weekend long commemorations. George not alone made all the necessary arrangements but lead the group.

The images below show George handing over the standard to Monsieur Frédéric Loinard, the Mayor of Colleville-Montgomery; the standard is now housed in the Mairie of Colleville-Montgomery.

Prior to the laying down of the standard there was a commemorative service with wreath laying at the statue of Field Marshall Bernard Law Montgomery. This would be the last use of the standard.

A plaque commemorating the event was unveiled nearby at the Office de Tourisme / Tourism Office; George undertook the Ceremony with Frédéric Loinard, Mayor and his Deputy, Isabelle Mevel.

George's speech at the laying down of the Standard,
Colleville-Montgomery, April 14th, 2018.

Mr. Mayor, Members of Colleville Council and Dignitaries, Veterans, Ladies and Gentlemen.
What a pleasure it is to be at Colleville-Montgomery today and be in the Company of so many of the friends we have made over the years.
Seventy four years ago at this time, we Normandy Veterans having completed months of trai9ning, were travelling all over the United Kingdom to Airfields, Naval Bases, Barracks and Camps in readiness to partake in the biggest invasion ever experienced. After a delay because of the weather, the big event commenced on the night of June 5th and daybreak on June 6th, 1944. Some 6,000 ships, hundreds of aircraft, some 200,000 servicemen and many tons of equipment were about to land on the coast of Normandy and, as history now shows, some months later had successfully rid Europe of the oppression and brutality that had been experienced over the previous six years. Sad to say on the initial invasion on D-Day over the three beaches, Gold, Juno and Sword, approximately 4,500 members of the British, Commonwealth and French Forces lost their lives. In addition, many more were lost on the American Beaches, Omaha and Utah. Before the Campaign that followed – until Normandy was completely liberated at the end of August, a total of approximately 21,500 military lives had been lost plus, of course, many more thousands of French civilian lives.
A terrible price to pay.
It must be remembered that the conflict was still operating in the Far East and more loves being lost on that Theatre. Many of the Servicemen who served in Normandy and the European Campaign subsequently were drafted to the Middle and Far East until the complete cessation of Worldwide hostilities in August 1945.
After all the Servicemen had returned home came the necessity of endeavouring to commence family life. Emotional reunions, obtaining employment, housing, accommodation, raising families etc – very often far more difficult that one now imagine. Thus, many of us were doing our best to forget the horrors of war we had experienced but missing the comradeship and friendships formed during our Service years intending for them to continue but inevitably all these good intentions fell by the wayside.
However, in 1981 in Cleethorpes on the Humber Estuary in Lincolnshire, four Normandy Veterans got together, and after many difficulties had been overcome, managed to form the nucleus of an Association which would eventually become the Normandy Veterans Association. The Association would grow to 105 Branches with representation in Australia, Belgium, Canada, France, Holland and Ireland with a membership exceeding 15,000. This gradually progressed to members attending Parades and Services in many places in the U.K., Belgium, France and Holland. Like all Regimental Associations, the tradition of having a standard for Parade, was adopted, one being designed. Eventually very Branch on formation were obliged to have their own standard with the same design as the original but with the name of the Branch and number. This then was paraded at local and national events. This was quite a sight to behold at National events with upwards of 80 – 90 Standards on parade and several thousand Veterans marching behind with their medals shining on their chest.
In 1946 the then town Council of Colleville asked Field Marshall Montgomery if he would accept the town changing their name from Colleville-sur-Orne to Colleville-

From left, Senator Sonia de la Provoté, Frédéric Loinard, Mayor, Guy Legrand, former Mayor and George. [image courtesy of Ouest-France]

Montgomery. This was in honour of the contribution made to ensure freedom. This was readily agreed to. Later, the town allowed us to erect a statute to the Field Marshall on land provided at no charge.

However, it was only when the Normandy Veterans Association was formed in 1981 that the wonderful relationship of the townspeople with Veterans realised. Since 1982 we have visited Colleville-Montgomery every year to hold a parade and service at Monty's Statue and afterwards, attend the Vin d'Honneur provided by the Mayor and Council.

There have been memorable occasions with upwards of 4,000 – 5,000 in attendance at the annual Ceremony. At times the road between La Plage and Monty's Statue was a sea of Standards and Veterans marching behind a band. We are now down to a few hundred but all those who have passed to Higher Service are in our memories when we are there.

For many years the Ceremony was organised by the National Committee but since the disbanding of the National Association, the responsibility has been proudly undertaken by South Eastern Branch. During this time we have engaged the West Yorkshire Police Band and the Dutch Liberation Band and introduced the now popular singer Emma Brown but most of all the Honourable Henry Montgomery, Monty's grandson to the Veterans and those in attendance.

Now is the time for our Branch to bid farewell to the Mayor and Committee Members, the towns people of Colleville-Montgomery, the memories of past events but most of all our friends and comrades we have left behind in the cemeteries throughout Normandy and those who marched with us in Remembrance and Commemoration.

We will never forget them, and kindness shown to us by everybody in Colleville-Montgomery.

'Thank you everyone' seems so inadequate but it is heartfelt.

*Commemor-
ations were
also held at
Chouain.*

*With wreaths
being laid to
those killed as a
result of friendly
fire in June
1944*

Jerusalem Cemetery has special connections with the South East Branch, being visited in the annual June visit. The Cemetery is the sole CWGC in the Chouain area.

Jerusalem Cemetery.......

To commemorate the links between the Branch and the Chouain Commune a standard was given to the three 'local' Mayors.

June 5th – the annual commemoration at Colleville-Montgomery; much was said of the laying down of the standard and of George by the Mayor, Frédéric Loinard, in his address to those gathered for the event. The standard was to the fore of all the standard on the day being proudly held by former Mayor of Colleville-Montgomery, Guy Legrand.

Guy Legrand, Maire honoraire, Colleville-Montgomery holds the Standard with pride.

Normandy 2018

George spent several weeks in Normandy in 2018 from Easter onwards; far from slowing down it seems the pace of Commemoration and Remembrance continues to accelerate. George is high in demand and this is most noticeable when events are being planned – not simply a case of turning up on the day, the necessary planning has to be made.

After the laying down of the standard, Number 23 Branch, at Colleville-Montgomery at Easter George was back in Normandy in early June for a series of Commemorative events. For the first time the Commemorative Ceremony and Service at Ravenoville was to have a British presence with George being that presence. This required an initial visit and introduction to the co-hosts of the Ceremony – David A. Ashe and Céline Lautour Schwab. George proved the centre of attention onsite and offsite – he was stopped by re-enactors for a long conversation!

The 'Eternal Heroes Memorial', Ravenoville.

During the Ceremony he sat beside several important dignitaries amongst who was Susan Eisenhower. George was particularly impressed with receiving a flag and plaque from Brigadier General K. Todd Royar, Deputy Commander 101St Airborne. After the Ceremony George attended another Ceremony required of all veterans visiting the site – signing the wall! His signature is in good company as directly above and to the right are the signatures of legendary D-Day Airborne soldiers – Bob Noody, 506th, 101St A/B, Bill Sullivan 505th, 82nd A/B and Dan McBride, 502nd, 101St A/B.

From Ravenoville on June 4th it was Bayeux on June 6th; the weather had turned from the warm and sunny day that was the 4th to a cool, misty and damp 6th.

A subsequent visit to Ravenoville followed in August as plans for the 2019 Ceremony there were formalised between Dave Ashe and George. The event gets bigger and bigger year to year.

In September George was part of a group of Veterans taken to Normandy on a Royal British Legion organised Tour. Based in Caen the group travelled to some seldom visited sites and Memorials.

Ravenoville (Manche)

Ravenoville village (Bourg) is a small commune situated four miles north-east of Ste Mère Eglise and less than two miles from the sea - the Bay of the Seine.

In June 1944, Ravenoville was occupied by the 4th Company of Grenadier-Regiment 919, 709th (Static) Infantry Division, commanded by an Oberleutnant Werner. The German HQ (Ortskommandantur) was the centuries-old Marmion Farm, a natural stone fortress with a quadrangle courtyard which dominates the important crossroads just south of the village leading north to Cherbourg, south to Carentan, east to Utah Beach and west to Ste Mère Eglise. Ravenoville was designated Wn11a (Wiederneststand, or resistance nest) on German maps, one of a series of strongpoints along the length of the eastern Cherbourg peninsula.

On D-Day, Ravenoville was just beyond the northern limit of the planned area of operations for the 101st Airborne Division, and approximately two miles from the 502nd Parachute Infantry Regiment's Drop Zone (DZ) 'A' at St Martin de Varreville. Minutes after 1.00am on D-Day morning, at least two mis-dropped 502nd sticks landed in the vicinity of Ravenoville. A further group of approximately fifteen 502nd paratroopers (also mis-dropped, near Ste Mère Eglise), commanded by Major John P. Stopka - Executive Officer (second in command) of 3rd Battalion, 502nd - arrived at the crossroads with the intention of turning right (south) to reach DZA. The paratroopers came under fire from the German garrison in the farm, so Stopka ordered six men led by 1Lt Ernest O. Harris to make a reconnaissance of the farm to establish the enemy strength. Harris divided his men into two squads of three, flanking right and left. Harris attacked a German trench system, personally killing six and taking twenty-four prisoners. The audacity of the surprise attack quickly persuaded the other Germans to surrender.

For his personal leadership and heroism, Ernest Harris was awarded a posthumous Distinguished Service Cross, the second highest American military award for gallantry. Harris was killed in action five days later at Carentan, he didn't live to learn of the recommendation (written two days after his death) or receive the award.

Major Stopka decided to hold the farm until relief arrived from Utah Beach, denying the enemy control of the crossroads and any attempt to attack the exposed northern limit of the airborne bridgehead less than a mile south at Foucarville.

A second group of approximately thirty Company A, 506th paratroopers led by 2Lt William W. Muir reached the eastern limit of Ravenoville before 9.00am on D-Day morning. They attacked through the village, clearing any remaining Germans house-by-house before reaching the high ground at the Church of St Gilles and Ravenoville Château where they linked with Stopka's men holding a perimeter in front of the farm.

Throughout D-Day, Stopka's hold on the farm strengthened with the arrival of further mis-dropped 101st paratroopers from the 502nd and 506th Regiments, the 377th Parachute Field Artillery Battalion, and even one stick from the 82nd Airborne's 508th Regiment.

Stopka's men held firm, isolated and surrounded, for 30 hours until a patrol from the 4th Infantry Division's 1st Battalion, 22nd Infantry Regiment reached the farm at 7.50am on the morning of June 7th. The link-up between the airborne and seaborne invaders was secured. The 22nd Infantry relieved the paratroopers, who began migrating south to their assigned drop zones and their units.

Ravenoville Plage (Beach) and Grand Hameau des Dunes, less than two miles from Ravenoville Bourg, was designated Wn13.

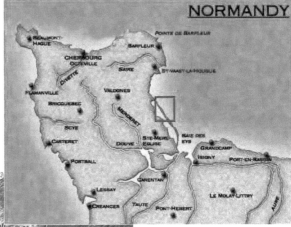

NORMANDY

It was defended by 4./919 Grenadier Regiment, 709th ID. 1.K.p./Bau.Pioneer Bt1. 59 I.D. And comprised –
2 x Vf2a crew bunkers.
1 x SK/Doppelschartenstand.
1 x Bf58c Tobruk.
1 x Vf Pakstand.
1 x 5cm KwK L/60.
1 x 4.7cm Pak 181(f).

Wn13 today – minus the roof and walls, leaving just the floor.

While the 22nd Infantry Regiment's 1st and 2nd Battalions pushed through Ravenoville to attack the powerful German coastal artillery batteries at St Marcouf and Azeville, the 3rd Battalion had the difficult assignment of reducing the German beach defences along the coast road, one-by-one, supported by amphibious (Duplex Drive) Sherman tanks. On D-Day evening the GI's were halted by German resistance more than a mile from Grand Hameau at Hameau des Cruttes. The attack resumed on June 7th, by-passing Hameau des Cruttes. That evening, a German prisoner persuaded the eighty-two German defenders holding out at Ravenoville Plage to surrender. Ravenoville was free after almost four long years of German occupation! - Courtesy David Ashe.

142

Above – George visiting David Ashe and Céline Lautour Schawab at Ravenoville, June 3rd, getting his instructions for the ceremony on June 4th. The lady between George and David is Madame Louisette Leducq, Secretary of the Friends of American Veterans Association.

below – George deep in conversation with Joe McCabe and other re-enactors, Ravenoville, June 3rd.

Presentation to George, Ravenoville, June 4th, 2018.

David Ashe and Céline Lautour Schwab organisers of the Commemoration at Ravenoville.

Above – George, front row – third left with American Veterans and current 101ˢᵗ servicemen and women at the Memorial in Ravenoville.

below – George with Susan Eisenhower before the Ceremony/Service at Ravenoville.

Signing the wall after the Ceremony/Service

The Service at Bayeux Cemetery, June 6th –
Cool, misty and damp.

George visiting David Ashe at Ravenoville, August, 2018 –

Visiting the display room and looking at the amazing diorama of the Marmion Farm, 1944.

Marmion Farm

Many famous photographs in D-Day and WWII books were taken at this site, where troopers gathered after they landed in Normandy.

At 0110, June 6th, 1944, Pfc Forrest 'Goody' L. Guth jumped over Normandy. An interview done sixty years later explains much of the importance of Marmion Farm - *The best 'Easy Company' could pull together after the jump was around a dozen men - our Coy, 1st Lt. T. Meehan III, O-437484, and most of HQ personnel never reported to the assembly area and were not seen again* (Aircraft 66 was hit by flak and crashed, killing all its 21 occupants). *I landed in a cow pasture, about 3 miles off target, somewhere between Ravenoville and the beach, and around dawn ran into more men from my stick. After trying to figure out what to do, we started moving toward Ravenoville searching for the rest of 'Easy'. At the southern edge of the village stood a 'square' farmhouse used by the Germans* (Marmion Farm), *the four of us, together with stragglers from different outfits and under leadership of Major John P. Stopka, 3rd Bn, 502nd PIR* (later to be killed in action during the Battle of the Bulge on January 14th, 1945), *captured the stronghold - that's the place where the 101st Airborne displayed the first nazi flag captured by our Division!* Just hours after the D-Day invasion began, James Flanagan with other paratroopers of the 101st Airborne Division, captured a Nazi flag from a command post headquarters in the farm complex. The paratroopers had landed in the middle of the night to eliminate German resistance along the causeways to Utah Beach.

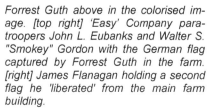

Forrest Guth above in the colorised image. [top right] 'Easy' Company paratroopers John L. Eubanks and Walter S. "Smokey" Gordon with the German flag captured by Forrest Guth in the farm. [right] James Flanagan holding a second flag he 'liberated' from the main farm building.

James Flanagan parachuted into Normandy hours before the U.S. Army's 4th Infantry Division was to land at Utah Beach on June 6th, 1944. He and his fellow airborne soldiers came down in the middle of the night, charged with removing any German resistance along the vulnerable causeways that led inland from the beach. They would be the prelude to the largest amphibious invasion in history.

After landing near Ravenoville, France, the first vehicle that the paratrooper saw later in the morning while mopping up near a captured farm complex was coming from the beach and carrying two men, one an International News Service photographer. It was 9 a.m., about three hours into 'the Longest Day' in history. The soldiers took a brief timeout so that the photographer could record the event. Flanagan, in the center, smiled while clutching the Nazi flag that had been 'liberated' from the enemy command post headquarters in the farm complex they now occupied. When this picture was wired back to the States, it became one of the most widely distributed newspaper photos taken from the events of June 6th.

James Flanagan was also interviewed - *Using my clicker* [cricket], *I started looking for company. At first I didn't recognize my position from the maps that I had previously studied. I heard some shooting, so I began moving toward Ravenoville. The firing was coming from a German MG42 machine gun. The person pulling the trigger, however, wasn't a very good shot. The Army had trained me how to crawl so that I was only 4 inches off the ground, so I did. Soon there was more activity. I began recognizing the sounds of our M-1s.*

By way of moonlight, using my clicker, I began joining up with troops from other companies and regiments. By dawn, there were about 20 of us. We didn't know each other, but a major [Major John P. Stopka, 3/502nd] *came over and organized us into a group and led us on an attack of a German garrison at a farm complex [Marmion] at Ravenoville. This was also the location of the German MG42 that had been firing on us. The Germans were about platoon size in strength. The battle lasted for about an hour and a half. Once the farm complex was captured, the major had us running patrols around the outlying areas in order to keep the Germans from sneaking up on us. We maintained outposts and patrols until we were relieved later in the day. We also had a dozen prisoners who we had to contend with. By noon, the 4th Infantry Division had* arrived from Utah Beach, and we were relieved. I spent the night of June 6 at Ravenoville.

By June 7th, I was back with my regiment and company, where I was assigned to patrols in and around the 502nd's areas of responsibility in Normandy near Houseville. We would patrol the area and try to clean out remaining German defenders. We ran around the bush. They ambushed us, and we ambushed them. This went on for several days.

David Ashe – Details of Flanagan's account is incorrect. No vehicle or other non-paratrooper appeared at the farm before 7.50am on June 7th. The iconic Flanagan photo was taken by Reuben Weiner, the Signal Corps photographer who jumped with the 82nd Airborne stick that wound up at the farm. The photo is a 'still' lifted from a short newsreel shot by Weiner on June 7th, not D-Day. Flanagan's date of relief as noon on D-Day is also incorrect. Again, 7.50am on D+1.

Ravenoville;
Location of the Memorial [top arrow] and the Marmion Farm [lower arrow].

Above – George taking a stroll along the seafront at Asnelles with Catherine Murphy; it was here that George came ashore in the early hours of D-Day some 74 years earlier, August 2018.

below – George relaxing with David Ashe overlooking Omaha Beach, August 2018.

Royal British Legion organised Tour, September 2018;

At Jerusalem Cemetery explaining why George chose this venue to be visited and be on the itinerary.

Royal British Legion organised Tour, September 2018;

Once a Royal Engineer, always a Royal Engineer; the three veterans on the Tour who served with the Royal Engineers at the R.E Memorial on the heights overlooking Arromanches.

Royal British Legion organised Tour, September 2018;

At Bayeux Cemetery – the twelve Normandy Veterans pose for the camera, above and below, George exiting the Cemetery deep in conversation.

THE BRITISH NORMANDY MEMORIAL

The Concept of a Memorial commemorating all those who served under British Command and who lost their lives in the Normandy Campaign, 1944 was one that George long thought of. Having spent several years pondering on the idea George finally got the required support he sought when the then Prime Minister, the Hon. David Cameron and the Chancellor of the Exchequer, the Hon. George Osborne agreed to support the concept.

Mr Cameron immediately agreed with George that a Memorial was not alone long overdue but was also very necessary. The change of Prime Minister did not in any way affect the original decision made by Mr Cameron and so the government lead by Mrs Theresa May accepted the Concept and a grant of £20,000,000 was given to ensure the success of the project.

Since then the original group of Trustees has expanded in number and George has accepted the role of Patron. After initial surveys it was agreed that the Memorial be built at Ver-sur-Mer rather than Colleville-Montgomery. The site at Ver-sur-Mer overlooks Gold Beach with the remains of the Mulberry at Arromanches to the left.

There are six trustees with The Lord Ricketts GCMG, GCVO the Chairman. The other Trustees are The Rt. Hon. The Lord Janvrin GCB, GCVO, QSO, General The Lord Dannatt GCB, CBE, MC, DL, General Sir Peter Wall GCB, CBE, DL, FR Eng, David McDonough OBE, Sir Michael Rake KBE, Mr Andrew Whitmarsh and Nicholas Witchell.

HRH, The Prince of Wales is the Royal Patron.

With Government backing it was now a case of building a team that would see the concept bear fruition and see the construction of the Memorial. Among those George sought help from was the eminent journalist and BBC Correspondent, Nicholas Witchell -

I first met George in the late summer of 2014. At the time I was the BBC radio commentator for the Ceremony of Remembrance at the Cenotaph. A principal focus that year was the 70th anniversary of D-Day. As part of the live transmission from the Cenotaph we collected a selection of recordings from veterans and others talking about their experiences and why remembrance mattered to them.

I drove down to meet George at his house in Kent to record his recollections of D-Day. I recall a big man, quietly spoken but self-evidently very focussed on the interests of the Normandy Veterans. He had for some years been the National Secretary of the Normandy Veterans' Association. A decision had been taken to disband the association so that year's Cenotaph ceremony would be their last parade in Whitehall: "it's sad and in a way heart-breaking" he told me "but although we won't be marching at the Cenotaph again our thoughts will still be there."

On Remembrance Sunday the small group of Normandy Veterans, led by George, had been given a position of prominence at the head of the march past, just behind all the officials of The Royal British Legion. I'd had a hand in persuading the Legion to move them up from their allocated place in view of the significance of the anniversary and the fact that this would be the last time the Normandy Veterans would appear. There was some resistance but in the end the Legion agreed that an exception should be made.

Perhaps that played some part in what followed, because about ten months later George and his friend Alastair Dutch, a retired diplomat, came up to London to see me. Alastair said they "wanted some advice." We met at the Reform Club. And it was there that George looked me in the eye and said there was a wrong that he wanted to put right.

"The Americans have got a national memorial in Normandy. The Canadians have got a memorial, but the British haven't," he said. It was such a simple, blindingly obvious point. I thought for a moment and realised that, yes, the British - alone among the principal wartime Allies - did not have a memorial in Normandy which recorded the names of all those who lost their lives on D-Day and in the weeks that followed.

And that's how it all started: over lunch at the Reform Club. "Let's see what we can do" was the thrust of what I told George and Alastair. A letter was drafted for George to send to the then Prime Minister David Cameron. They'd met at the ceremonies in Normandy to mark the 70th anniversary and Mr Cameron had told George "if there's ever anything you want George, just get in touch."

Fine words which no doubt were sincerely meant when they were uttered. But George's letter to Mr Cameron went unanswered for fully three months. And when, after a reminder, a reply did arrive it had obviously been drafted by a middle-ranking civil servant. It was full of warm words about how much the veterans were valued – "The Normandy Veterans are among the bravest of the many who fought and died" the letter said – but there was nothing of real significance in terms of building a memorial to them.

However by then I'd made contact with the man – a Captain in the Royal Navy – who at that time was serving as an adviser to the then Chancellor of the Exchequer, George Osborne. This official, who would be embarrassed if I were to name him, deserves very considerable credit for everything that has followed.

He got it: he immediately saw the merit of what we were proposing. To cut a long story short: I set up the Normandy Memorial Trust; approached our architect Liam O'Connor – designer among other things of the Bomber Command Memorial in Green Park London (he too "got it" immediately); we searched for a site -- a number were examined and rejected as being unsuitable before, on 12th September 2017, we found our site overlooking 'Gold Beach' at Ver-sur-Mer. As soon as Liam and I saw it we knew that this had to be the place where the British Normandy Memorial should be constructed.

In the meantime we had secured a grant of £20 million from the Treasury's LIBOR fund, financed by the fines imposed on City institutions which had broken the rules.

It has been quite a task, but I will say without hesitation that it is the most worthwhile thing I have done in my so-called "career".

The dream of George Batts and the other veterans whom it has been my privilege to meet over the past four years – men like the redoubtable Harry Billinge, Joe Cattini, Ronald Clements, Jim Radford, Lord Edwin Bramall and many others – will become a reality.

The British Normandy Memorial will be built, on a hillside overlooking the "Gold Beach" where George and so many other brave men came ashore on the morning of 6th June 1944 -- and it will record the names of the 22,442 men and women who never came home.

Image courtesy Normandy Memorial Trust

Unveiling the site to the Veterans

On June 6th, 2018 several of the Trustees, members of the Public and a number of Normandy Veterans travelled to the site where the Memorial will stand. Nicholas Witchell warmly greeted everyone in a marquee erected for the occasion – a most welcome cover as the afternoon was quite windy! For George as Patron this was reality – he was standing on the very site the Memorial will be.

Above – George takes the plaudits at the unveiling of the concept on the very Memorial site at Ver-sur-Mer, June 6th, 2018.

below – Nicholas Witchell speaking with George outside the marquee.

An exceptional brochure was available on the day; the brochure is extensive in its detail of the design and background to the Memorial.

George contributed to the brochure advertising the Memorial –

It has been my dream for many years that a Memorial be built in Normandy to record the names of all the British servicemen and women and those from the civilian services who lost their lives in the D-Day landings and the Normandy Campaign. The Americans have a memorial at Omaha and the Canadians a memorial on Juno. It is not right that the Brits do not have a similar memorial. When the Normandy Veterans Association disbanded in 2014 and I stepped down as National Secretary I was determined to raise the money to build a memorial to all the mates we left behind. The British government has given us a fantastic start in funding terms - but to deliver the complete memorial project to match those of other nations we will need to go further. It is my greatest wish and that of other Veterans to see this project completed in our lifetimes. If the remembrance of what was done on the D-Day beaches matters to you we would be so grateful for your support. In the name of the Normandy Veterans, thank you.

George Batts MBE Leg d'Hon Patron
The Normandy Memorial Trust

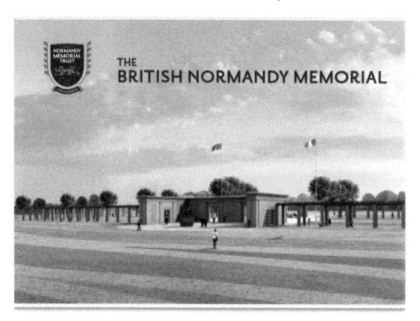

Images courtesy Normandy Memorial Trust.

THE DUTY OF REMEMBRANCE

The task of commemorating those who fell during D-Day and the Battle of Normandy does not end with the construction of the British Normandy Memorial.

The Duty of Remembrance continues. The Normandy Memorial Trust wishes to ensure that the generations of the future understand why these men and women were prepared to sacrifice their lives - and what they achieved by doing so.

An Education Centre will be an interactive space designed to bring to life the stories of those who did their duty in Normandy in the summer of 1944.

It is an inspiring story, underpinned by the long association of two of Europe's great nations, the United Kingdom and France.

In the next phase of the Memorial project the Trust will work with historians and educational experts to create both a physical and virtual space to tell visitors about the lead-up to D-Day, the gathering of the Allied forces, the contribution of the "Home Front" in Britain, the vital role of the French Resistance and the resilience of the French civilian population.

Above all, the visitors of tomorrow should be helped to understand the leading contribution made by the United Kingdom alongside its wartime allies to secure the freedom of Europe.

The Trust will seek funding for an Education Centre from private and corporate sources and hopes to open it in time for the 80th anniversary of D-Day in 2024.

A view of the proposed Education Centre

D Day Veteran George Batts was an 18 year old Sapper when he landed on Gold Beach on the morning of D Day itself. Tasked with clearing mines and booby traps he survived the horrors of the beaches while many of his friends and comrades tragically died.

George who eventually became the National Secretary of the Normandy Veterans Association has long held an ambition that a defining monument should be built on a single site in France to commemorate the men and women of the British Armed forces and civilian services who lost their lives in the Normandy Campaign.

The Normandy Memorial Trust, harnessing George's remarkable tenacity and long held passion, has secured a commitment from the UK Government to construct a powerful and inspiring statement which will endure in Normandy to honour the fallen.

Above – Nicholas Witchell explain some of the finer points to Catherine Murphy in the marquee.

Below – George explaining the concept of the Memorial.

The message George sent to the Commissioner who was compiling comments, Public Enquiry, December 2018/February 2019.

January 21st 2019

Monsieur Deneux,

I have been visiting Normandy every year in early June since the 50th Anniversary of the débarquement en Normandie in 1994. Over these past 24 years - 25 years this coming June - I have made many friends in Normandy. I have always been made most welcome by the people of Normandy who will always express their gratitude and thanks for what was done that Summer in 1944. I look on Normandy as a second home whenever I have the opportunity to visit which is not just in early June. My visits always include Colleville-Montgomery and Arromanches, Jerusalem Cemetery and Bayeux Cemetery to name a few places.

I never thought this would be the case when I came ashore as a [Special Forces] Engineer in the early hours of June 6th, 1944 at Asnelles on what was Gold Beach. I have forgotten much of what happened that day other than the casualties as they quickly mounted. Over the following weeks I was working on the Harbour in Arromanches assisting with the constant movement of men and equipment and supplies coming in to the Front and the movement of the wounded going back to England. I lost many friends over those weeks of the Bataille de Normandie, many now buried in Bayeux.

It is in this context that I am writing to you.

As a former Committee Member of the National Executive of the Normandy Veterans' Association I have strived to promote the memory of those servicemen and women who served with the British Armed Services [to include commando Kieffer]. I was recognized by M. Nicolas Sarkozy, Président de la République, in 2009 for these efforts and in the promotion of Anglo-French relations in Normandy through the award of the Légion d'Honneur. Three years ago I spoke to Mr David Cameron, Prime Minister, of my concept of creating a Memorial to commemorate all those servicemen who served with the British Armed Services - a truly international group comprising not only British and French but also Irish, Belgian, Dutch [and more] servicemen and women. Mr Cameron thoroughly backed the concept as does his successor Mrs Theresa May.

I remain committed to the concept and know the people of Normandy support the creation of this Memorial.

I speak on behalf of all Normandy Veterans and all our friends both here in England and in Normandy in the propped building of the Memorial.

22,442 SACRIFICE FOR FREEDOM CAMPAIGN LAUNCH

The Campaign was launched at the National Army Museum on February 7th, 2019. Seven Veterans of the Normandy Campaign were guests of honour as the Trust introduced the project to over 250 distinguished guests.
George was interviewed [and recorded] on arrival at the National Army Museum.

George Batts MBE, Leg d'Hon
Patron

The guests of Honour – the nine Normandy Veterans.
Images courtesy Normandy Memorial Trust.

Above - Veterans left to right Jim Radford, Ronald Clements, George Simms, George Batts, Joe Cattini, Harry Billinge, Field Marshal Lord Edwin Bramall.

below – Nicholas Witchell at the podium with George's 'banner' to his right.
Images courtesy Normandy Memorial Trust.

Above - Field Marshal Lord Edwin Bramall with George,

below – Field Marshal Lord Edwin Bramall is momentarily distracted as George and Jim Radford pose for the camera.

Above – George with the Hon. Henry Montgomery, Edward Llewellyn, Baron Llewellyn of Steep, HM Ambassador to France and Joe Cattini.

below – George taking applause for instigating the project.
Image courtesy Normandy Memorial Trust.

Acknowledgements

There has been a most welcome response from everyone contacted to provide material, guidance and advice not to mention corrections to compile this biography.

The students of The History Society, St John's Catholic School, Gravesend who had the concept and the 6th Formers who interviewed George and undertook the work in creating the book. Matt Barron, Headteacher and Dan Walton, Associate Headteacher for their support with the project.

Paul Foster who ensured the book was printed and published and who created the covers.

Photographs and information have been forthcoming from the Australian War Museum, the Cowfold Historical Society, the Jockey Club. Horsham Football Club and the Commonwealth War Graves Commission.

The Foreign and Commonwealth Office was most obliging in forwarding communications and a thank you too to Alistair Dutch for assisting with emails.

The Hon. Henry Montgomery who most generous in their contributions and support as were David Ashe 'Irish Dave' and Céline Lautour-Schwab of Ravenoville and Frédéric Loinard and Isabelle Mevel, Colleville-Montgomery. David corrected material in Chapter 5.

A sincere thank you to Caroline and Colin of Aces High, Wendover and Ste Mère Église, for their continuing support and enthusiasm.

The Normandy Memorial Trust provided several images for Chapter 6 and a sincere thank you to Nicholas Witchell for his lengthy contribution in that Chapter, clearly and succinctly summing up how ideas flowed from concept and to fruition.

Proceeds of this book go directly to the Normandy Memorial fund.

George at an Aces High event at Wendover with Caroline Fowler, Manager.

At Jerusalem Cemetery, Chouain.